SpringerBriefs in Business

SpringerBriefs present concise summaries of cutting-edge research and practical applications across a wide spectrum of fields. Featuring compact volumes of 50 to 125 pages, the series covers a range of content from professional to academic. Typical topics might include:

- A timely report of state-of-the art analytical techniques
- A bridge between new research results, as published in journal articles, and a contextual literature review
- A snapshot of a hot or emerging topic
- An in-depth case study or clinical example
- A presentation of core concepts that students must understand in order to make independent contributions

SpringerBriefs in Business showcase emerging theory, empirical research, and practical application in management, finance, entrepreneurship, marketing, operations research, and related fields, from a global author community.

Briefs are characterized by fast, global electronic dissemination, standard publishing contracts, standardized manuscript preparation and formatting guidelines, and expedited production schedules.

More information about this series at http://www.springer.com/series/8860

Shigeo Atsuji

Resilience Management for a Sustainable Aging Society

Preventability of Medical Accidents Using Big Data

 Springer

Shigeo Atsuji
Kansai University
Kyoto, Japan

ISSN 2191-5482   ISSN 2191-5490 (electronic)
SpringerBriefs in Business
ISBN 978-981-13-5804-3   ISBN 978-981-13-5805-0 (eBook)
https://doi.org/10.1007/978-981-13-5805-0

Library of Congress Control Number: 2019933192

This Springer imprint is published by the registered company Springer Nature Singapore Pte Ltd.
The registered company address is: 152 Beach Road, #21-01/04 Gateway East, Singapore 189721, Singapore

To my family.

Preface: Resilience Management for Medical Sustainability

The origins of this book lie in the world congress of the International Society for the Systems Sciences (ISSS) held at Vienna Technical University from July 9 to 14, 2017, during which, in the framework of Workshop 3241: Strengthening the Resilience of Aging Societies (chaired by S. Sankaran and G. Chroust; Room SR127), disaster reduction management to reduce medical accidents was proposed as a solution for 'resilience in the aged society.' In advance of this workshop, at the July 10 conference meeting of the Special Interest Group on Systematic Approaches to Conflict, the author had made a joint presentation of conference entitled Resilience Management: from Fukushima Disaster to Boiling Oceans and Viral Spread (Atsuji Shigeo; Chroust, Gerhard; Fujimoto, Ryosuke: Room: SR125) (conference item number 3194). Since 2011, the author had moreover been active in related presentations at the world congress of the ISSS and publications in academic journals. The author's research was originally viewed as heretical within Japan, but thanks in part to the guidance of Prof. G. Chroust (Disaster Management), the author continued, as a small contribution to the world's knowledge, with his research into modalities of management for the reduction of disasters and accidents, leading in 2016 to Springer's publication of the author's previous work: *Unsafety*: Disaster Management, Organizational Accidents and Crisis Sciences for Sustainability. In August 2017, a forerunner to the present work, co-authored with Gerhard Chroust, appeared in the ISSS Journal under the title Resilience Management: From Fukushima Disaster to Boiling Oceans and Northward Viral Spread.

Japan has always been exposed to an unparalleled level of natural disaster. In response to these national calamities, it has historically developed capabilities in disaster reduction that were unprecedented in human history. Japan's ability to adapt to natural disaster has attracted the attention of other countries around the world struggling with disasters of the same kind. Geographically, Japan is situated beside the world's largest ocean. In terms of its marine environment, warm sea currents from the equator and cold currents from the Sea of Okhotsk and the Arctic Ocean make for rich fishing grounds. Its atmospheric situation however brings strong winds and heavy rain including regular typhoons, and heavy snows along the Japan Sea coast. In geological terms, four of the plates of the earth's crust

(Eurasian, Pacific, North American, and Philippine) push up against each other in Japan, making it one of the world's most active earthquake zones. The country is thus exposed to all kinds of disaster, from earthquakes and tsunamis to typhoons and volcanic eruptions, floods and torrential rains. At least partly due to the impact of global warming, there has been a sharp rise in the frequency of great typhoons in proportion to the rise in seawater temperature. The increasing frequency of storms of high intensity (atmospheric pressure of 900 hectopascals or lower) and of large scale (diameter of 1000 km), together with hurricanes, cyclones, and tropical low pressure systems at high latitudes, has led to an expansion of the areas exposed to damage. It is therefore now time to re-assess our approach to major disasters, the reduction of which is a pressing concern. The time course of disaster is as follows:

(1) In advance: Risk Management
(2) During disaster: Crisis Management
(3) After disaster: Resilience Management

In recent years, studies have begun into the optimal distribution of resources to cope with risk, but are not yet sufficient in the areas of (2) and (3) above. Studies into disaster prevention have been ongoing, along with budgetary provisions for coastal levees and other measures. Preparations have nevertheless been inadequate, with no simulation of crisis management during disaster or post-disaster recovery measures. While the timing of a disaster is of course unknown, the cyclical nature of disaster means that a lasting record of damage spanning the generation is present everywhere. Natural disasters, which cannot be expounded scientifically with immediately available statistics, have been omitted as a subject of scientific inquiry on the basis of their unpredictability. However, this leaves the local communities and citizens who are the actual victims of disaster to face a tragic reality. People's sense of mourning at having lost family and friends, having lost all their possessions when their house was washed away, and having lost their work and even their community, is incomparably tragic. To prevent this greatest of misfortunes, we have fulfilled out citizens' duties and paid our taxes to contribute to central and local governments. Thus, to say that all natural and human disasters are 'unpredictable' is not a serious response.

Japan is not only susceptible to natural disaster, but also has many security holes that lead to human-made disaster. In geopolitical terms, with Russia to the north, China to the west, and America over the sea to the east, it is surrounded by great powers that have helped shape its eventful history. The tense situation in East Asia today around nuclear development, missile launches, and other security issues offers no guarantee of safety and stability.

Regarding the motive for publication, in response to the situation outlined above, the author has since the publication of the work entitled *Unsafety* (2016) been seeking concrete prescriptions to reduce world unsafety. Responding to the sharp rise in natural disasters caused by climate change, irregular weather patterns, and global warming, and to the increasing level of other global risks and crises, such as food and water shortages due to population explosion and refugee flows from war and terrorism, the author considered carefully the immediate tasks requiring the attention of the disaster reduction research teams of the International Society for the Systems Sciences. Considering the natural and human-made environments and their interaction, which were the issues within the context of global risk that were susceptible to improvement through everyday action and to which the systems approach method could be effectively applied? I attempted to highlight the positive and negative aspects of the self-inflicted situation of falling birth rates and social aging, which is affecting mainly the developed countries, and explored the possibility of social collapse. Especially in the developed countries, expenditure on the medical care of the elderly is placing an increasing burden on national budgets. In Japan for instance, current medical care expenditure stands at approximately 30 trillion yen and, according to the forecasts of the relevant government office, will surpass 50 trillion yen in the near future to reach 60 trillion yen, thus accounting for more than half of the national budget of approximately 100 trillion yen (general accounting calculation). Starting with the pension system, the nation's welfare foundations are being shaken in a shared crisis that is stealthily overtaking the advanced nations. Tax receipts and other income from the next generation, who are the children of the current elderly population, are the resources that support many of the nation's systems, including the pension system. However, the phenomenon of a reversed population structure has now brought about the increasingly widespread possibility of the collapse of these social systems. As a scholar of disaster reduction, what are the concrete prescriptions and ideas which the author can contribute to the world?

Already in Japan, the pension receipt age has been raised from 60 to 65 years or above, thus lengthening working life and delaying pension payment so as to secure the required capital resources. It is true that average life span and average survival after retirement have increased, but it is also necessary to take account of the number of years of healthy life when considering the appropriate length of working life. The fiscal burden of ever increasing medical care costs in the developed nations will fall in general on the public, including medical care stakeholders (patients and their families, medical care professionals, medical manufacturers, the pharmaceutical industry, the responsible government offices, etc.). As even healthy individuals who are currently not ill cannot exclude the possibility of hospitalization in the future due to illness or accident, in the end, medical care costs considered over the full span of a human life remain a public issue.

To prepare for the coming crisis in social welfare (welfare, public health, medical care, long-term care, retirement pension) by reducing, by however little, the risk presented by medical care expenditure in the near future, one urgent task is disaster reduction in the area of medical accidents, which impose a heavy burden on medical care stakeholders. Already, based on a study of medical care statistics, the Washington Post has cited medical accidents as the third greatest cause of death following heart disease and cancer. In the present publication, I am motivated by the wish to mitigate this trend, using tools of modern science such as big data and deep learning, artificial intelligence databases, nanotechnology, and new materials, by applying the concept of systems innovation and organizational reform to promote resilience management supported by information and communications technology as a move toward reducing medical accidents, and at the same time reducing similar accidents worldwide by means of a global database.

Acknowledgements

For the present publication, I received the recommendation of Prof. Dr. S. Sankaran, President of ISSS. I express thanks to Prof. Dr. G. Chroust (Austria), Prof. Dr. M Morley (Ireland), Prof. Dr. M. von Zedtwitz (Switzerland), Prof. Dr. P. Su (UK) and Prof. Dr. K. Hioki (Japan). For advice on the content of the medical accidents and the terminology used in the book, I thank MD/PhD. Y. Yasuda and the numerous other medical specialists who provided guidance. For assistance in the making of the book, I thank my collaborators T. Hannon, Y. Oya and K. Shinji, who provided English-language guidance. I am also grateful to doctoral student R. Fujimoto, with whose cooperation I undertook data mining of newspaper articles on Japanese medical accidents in the period from 2000 to 2016 to assemble a big-data database. For support in the publication process, I thank Springer editors Y. Hirachi, Parimelazhagan Thirumani, Megana Dinesh and S. Mimura. My thanks also to Kansai University for granting me a sabbatical and to MEXT KAKENHI (Grant Number 24530437).

Kyoto, Japan   Shigeo Atsuji
December 2018

Contents

About the Author

Dr. Shigeo Atsuji is Professor of Informatics at Kansai University in Japan and Research Fellow at Kyoto University (2012–2013). With a DBA in organization theory and a Ph.D. in policy sciences, he is a member of a number of scholarly associations and societies. Research interests focus on management informatics and organizational intelligence, decision-making theory, and the organizational aspects of accident and disaster, with an advisory board of KIRAS by FFG. He has presented associated case studies funded by the government at international conferences including those of International Federation of Scholarly Associations of Management (IFSAM) and the International Society for Systems Sciences (ISSS).

Springer publication: *UNSAFETY: Disaster Management, Organizational Accidents, and Crisis Sciences for Sustainability*, 2016.

List of Figures

List of Tables

Chapter 1
Resilience Management for Disaster Reduction Against Medical Accidents

1.1 Introduction

The publicizing of medical accidents as a social issue is the sign of a medically advanced nation accompanying the democratization of medical treatment. On the other hand, in countries with less developed medical treatment systems, there is a tendency for medical accidents not to be publicized. In Japan, programs of preventive mass immunization were carried out in the past, but as a result of using the same injection needle for a number of children, Japan now has an estimated 2–3 million people infected with hepatitis. In recent years, preventive medicines such as Tamiflu and preventive drugs against cervical cancer have come into widespread use, but the accompanying side effects have also become an urgent problem.

The preparation of big data on medical accidents in Japan (2000–2016) allows inference of past trends and tendencies in accidents, which can be fed back into the medical treatment policies of central government and administrative institutions and the public health practice of local government. Information on medical accidents is already published by the Japan Council for Quality Health Care, mainly through the Ministry of Health, Labour and Welfare (following MHLW). However, although detailed analysis has been undertaken of specific accident examples, it has been difficult to capture macro-trends across the range of accidents. The use of big data to socialize knowledge of failure for sharing by stakeholders, including medical personnel and patients, will support accident reduction in medical treatment. It is to be hoped that this will now usher in an age of 'ICT disaster management' for medical accident prevention.

1.2 International Definition of Medical Accidents and Errors

According to the Washington Post, medical accidents are the third greatest cause of death after stroke and cancer [1]. In his work 'Errors in Medicine,' Professor L. Leape demonstrates the need to prevent medical accidents and points to the increase in the number of accidents in the United States and Britain [2]. The number of medical accidents and medical errors in Japan in the 17 years from January 2000 to December 2016, counting only those reported in newspapers, was 439. America and Britain also report continually occurring medical accidents. In these medically advanced nations, there has been a shift to a policy of not concealing accidents, but instead seeking to improve the situation by making them public, thereby securing confidence in medical institutions. In Japan, proactive prevention initiatives against medical accidents and errors and other medical disasters have now been introduced by the MHLW, medical institutions and corporations, and other relevant bodies, and these measures include independently devised strategies. In the interest of medical accident prevention, the MHLW has presented a document entitled Comprehensive Strategy for Medical Safety Promotion: Advance Prevention of Medical Accidents, which is based on the Report of the Investigative Committee on Measures to Prevent Accidents caused by Patient Misidentification. With reference to the work of the medical accident researcher Lucian L. Leape and organizational accident researcher J. Reason's *The Human Contribution: Unsafe Acts, Accidents, and Heroic Recoveries* [3], the present book analyzes big data on medical accidents in Japan from 2000 to 2016 to investigate the potential for reducing the number of disasters with the help of information and communications technology (ICT). This research is intended not as a criticism of medical institutions and medical policy, but as a contribution toward reducing medical accidents in the near future.

1.2.1 Changing Attitudes to Medical Accidents and Difference in Concepts

In America, Britain, Japan, and other medically advanced nations, medical accidents are publicized and have become a social issue. In Japan, the number of medical accident-related lawsuits doubled between 1990 and 2000 from approximately 400 to approximately 800. According to a survey by L. Leape of Harvard University, the rate of occurrence of medical accidents is around 10%, and approximately 4% of patients suffer injury as a result of prescription, leading to death in approximately 14% of cases. In America, it is estimated that 1.3 million people suffer injury due to medical accidents every year, and 180,000 of them die, with two-thirds of the accidents classed as preventable cases of negligence [4].

Based on the results of this survey, the Institute of Medicine (National Academy of Medicine) in America published a report in 1999 which claimed that 44,000–98,000 patients a year die in medical accidents in America [5], and concluded that accidents arise from negligence and errors preventable through reform of medical institutions. In response to the above-mentioned Institute of Medicine report, initiatives to deal with medical accidents began in earnest in America, where research into medical safety measures is ongoing in the field of patient safety. In Britain also, the National Health Service (NHS) released a report in 2000 [6], an institution has been set up to gather accident data, and social initiatives to reduce accidents are in progress.

In Japan, accident prevention initiatives were launched in response to a medical accident in 2001, of which we will make a case study later. In 2002, the MHLW and the Japan Medical Association published accident prevention guidelines [7]. Regarding American and British initiatives for medical accident prevention and differences from Japan, let us start with a comparison to show the different definitions used in Japan and overseas in the terminological categories for medical accidents (Table 1.1).

Table 1.1 International comparisons of medical accident categories

Japan	USA
(i) **Medical accidents and medical errors** Medical accident is a comprehensive term which includes all case of personal injury arising at any stage in the medical treatment process at a location connected with medical treatment, whereas medical error refers to a case where patient injury results from a medical professional neglecting to exercise due care in the medical treatment process	(i) **Adverse event** Designates all injury occurring in any context relating to medical treatment, also manifest as damage or complications (a) *Preventable adverse event* Refers to injury arising from error or systemic failure Additionally classified into three types according to the agent
(ii) **Incident** Refers to a situation in the routine course of medical practice where the patient does not sustain injury, but a near miss or close call is experienced	• Type 1: error by the attending physician • Type 2: error by a member of the medical team other than a doctor • Type 3: systemic failure not involving individual error
(iii) **Error** A human action is classified as an error for instance where (1) it is not intended by the agent (2) it is undesirable with reference to regulations (3) it is undesirable from the viewpoint of a third party (4) it fails to satisfy objectively expected standards	(b) *Unpreventable adverse event* Injury not caused by error or systemic failure and that may not always be necessarily preventable even under application of the latest scientific knowledge • Type 1: High-risk treatment resulting in injury that occurs frequently and is well known
(iv) **Misunderstanding** Misunderstanding is a form of error in which something not actually present is thought to exist or something present is not correctly identified. This may for instance be the mishearing of verbal communication, misreading of written information or displays, misreading of data on instrumentation, misunderstanding in an accustomed operation, or misidentification of a patient. This may be the cause of a medical accident	• Type 2: Injury due to a risk known but occurring only rarely in normal medical practice. Includes side effects of drugs (ii) **Medical error** Failure to carry out the planned intervention in the intended fashion, or adoption of an erroneous plan to achieve the goal

(continued)

Table 1.1 (continued)

Japan	USA
	(iii) **Serious error**
	Error with the potential to cause injury which may result in lasting damage, or only temporary but potentially life-threatening damage
	(iv) **Minor error**
	Error that does not cause injury or without the potential to cause injury
	(v) **Near miss**
	Error which could cause injury but is intercepted before it can affect the patient
	(vi) **Incident**
	Also known as adverse event, serious error, or accident

Note Indicates that, in Japan, medical accident is the main term used in a wider sense, while medical error appears to be used in a narrower sense. In Europe and North America, medical accident categories are different: firstly, a distinction is made depending on whether the medical intervention results in adverse effect on the patient and secondly a distinction is made between preventable and unpreventable events depending on whether negligence is present. The present book adopts a definition of medical accident and error in accordance with the classification of the MHLW, but it is likely in future that the categorization of medical accidents will move toward an international standard

1.2.2 Medical Safety Management

According to a survey by L. Leape, of all medical accidents, 29% are accounted for by mistaken diagnoses, mistakes in treatment methods or prescriptions, and surgical mistakes and 19% by mistakes in drug administration [8]. Some issues relate to pharmaceutical drug management, for instance mistaken selection and administration due to storing of hazardous drugs in the same place as other drugs or to similarities in the color and design of pharmaceutical packages. Many medical professionals have experience of a medical accident, but few of those involved report it freely. Today, innovation in medical technology has placed team treatment in the mainstream, which means that a number of specialist doctors and nurses and engineers are involved in the treatment. If just one of them makes a mistake, there is an impact on the whole course of treatment, frequently resulting in accident. It is obvious that medical professionals also make mistakes, but if an accident does occur, there has been a tendency for doctors, nurses, and also the hospital authorities to cover up or misrepresent their own negligence, so that safety management to prevent recurrence of the same accident is not shared, which represents an underlying issue in the organizational culture.

This secrecy within the world of medicine is not limited to Japan but is also found in Europe and North America. D. Hilfiker describes in an article his experience of carrying out an abortion based on the diagnosis that the fetus was dead, but later discovering that it had been alive up to the time of the surgery. A mistaken diagnosis thus led to a medical accident and resulted in deep feelings of guilt and the anguish of being unable to confide in anyone [9]. It has been commented that doctors attempt to resolve issues within their own range of skills, which results in insufficient exchange with other doctors and with entities beyond the bounds of the hospital and insufficient communication within the team. In a survey by J. B. Sexton et al., whereas 80% of surgeons rated the teamwork during surgery as 'good,' the figure among anesthetists and nurses was 25–40%, indicating a gap in the perception of communication [10].

There were also issues with the internal reporting system. The 'three strikes and out' system, whereby a third mistake means dismissal, is one where reporting leads to attribution of individual responsibility. As a result, there is a tendency to perpetuate the cover-up of accidents. In order to learn from the tragedy of a medical accident, it is essential for this system that encourages silence to be reformed at organizational level, and desirable for medical professionals to share with others and draw lessons. Useful to that end is an anonymous reporting system involving a third-party organization, and introduction thereof is already advanced in Europe and North America.

In America, Britain, Germany, and other medically advanced nations, so as not to repeat the same accident in the clinical setting, there has been a shift from pursuing the responsibility for the accident to establishing the cause. In order to make up for unsuccessful teamwork and insufficient communication, R. Simon proposed corrective measures such as vocal confirmation, shared understanding between team members, and a system of double-checking for miscommunication [11]. These are 'medical safety management' techniques that have been used in the high-risk industries of aviation, rail, and nuclear power, suggesting that the medical world needs to use the range of safety management techniques accumulated by these industries. Meanwhile, the development of new treatment methods and new drugs accompanying the development of medical technology and instruments, along with innovations in biotechnology including ES cells and iPS drug discovery, have meant that the acquisition of knowledge and skills by medical professionals lags behind, leading to accidents in a considerable number of cases.

Medical advances have made possible the treatment of intractable diseases and early patient recovery, but advanced technology and instrumentation also contain risks and 'security holes' as in the Swiss-cheese model that make accidents more likely [12]. The increasing complexity of the instruments used in advanced medical treatment and the number of available drugs—now over 10,000 and constantly growing—are among the factors contributing to increasing division of labor among medical personnel and to the increasing range of tasks carried out by doctors, nurses, and medical engineers. Delivering treatment therefore requires a system for real-time specialist division of labor. Today, medical professionals are obliged to carry out a physically and mentally arduous task within which a variety of factors can be identified as leading to accidents, among them constantly advancing medical innovations, increasingly specialized division of testing and diagnosis systems, communication among team members in team treatment, coordination between different medical departments in the diagnosis and treatment of patients with complications, and the systems for medical treatment management deployed by hospital organizations, including management of information on medical professionals that is held by patients. Behind medical accidents and errors lie not only the human and organizational factors involved in the advanced medical treatment of modern times, but also systemic factors within these complex systems. Numerous frontline accidents occur not only at medical treatment institutions but also at long-term care and welfare facilities, and this will require attention going forward. In the next section, we present an analysis of data relating to medical accidents and errors occurring in Japan with a view to classification of accident cause.

1.3   Data Mining Using the Resource Japan Medical Accident Big Data 2000–16

1.3.1   Diversification of Medical Accidents and Errors

Using as data the list of accidents in the resource Japan Medical Accident Big Data 2000–16, we carried out a classification by accident cause in accordance with the MHLW's criteria for medical accidents, incidents, errors, misunderstandings, and other mistakes. However, the trend of accidents in recent years turns up frequent examples that do not fit into these categories. We therefore attempted a reclassification based on at least nine indicative factors. Fig. 1.1 is a graphic representation based on text-mining of unstructured data from newspaper articles arranged year by year by accident cause.

A: *Medical intervention*

Refers to diagnosis and surgical treatment, drug prescription or other action for the purpose of treatment of disease and injury. This includes for example direct surgical mistakes, cases where surgical gauze is inadvertently left in the body after an operation, or where injection is given at the wrong site.

B: *Nursing intervention*

Refers to the general range of nursing action to support the patient as an auxiliary to the above-mentioned medical intervention but excluding medical intervention. For example, cases where the wrong intravenous drip drug is administered or where an artificial respirator is inadvertently not connected to the power source.

C: *Patient action*

Refers to accidents arising from the patient own action. Includes, for example, falls in the hospital, falling out of bed, refusing medical intervention, violence against medical professionals, or other obstructive action. It additionally includes cases where the patient seeks a second opinion from one or more other medical institutions and is given a different prescription concurrently, resulting in problems caused by multi-drug co-medication unintended by the patient.

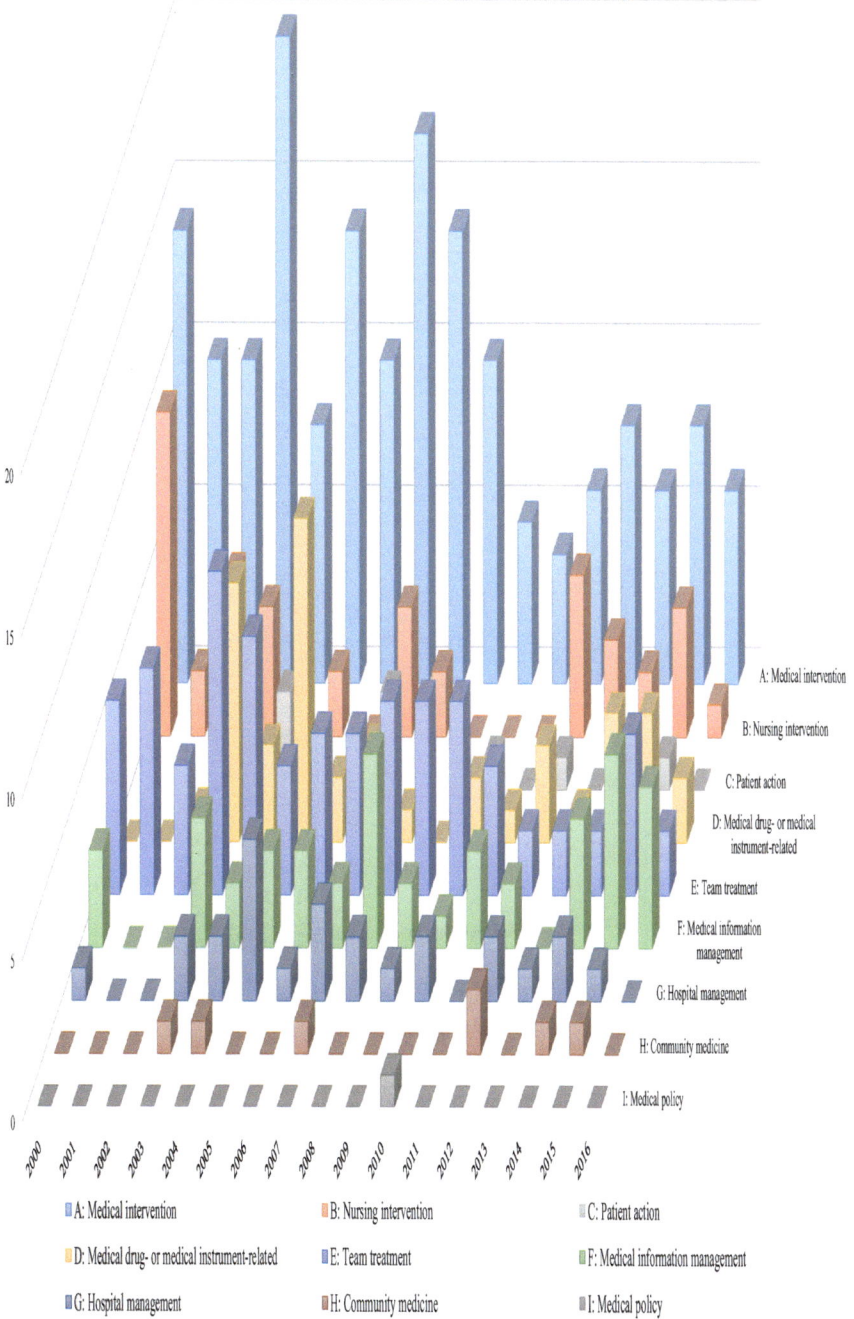

Fig. 1.1 Intermediate classifications of medical accidents: trend in number of events (Japan, 2000–16) by Atsuji Seminar. *Source* Medical Accidents 2000–16: Statistical Trends by Cause of Accident [3D graphic representation using below Table 1.2]

Table 1.2 2000–16 Statistical trend in medical accidents

	2000	2001	2002	2003	2004	2005	2006	2007	2008	2009	2010	2011	2012	2013	2014	2015	2016	Total
A: Medical intervention	14	10	10	20	8	14	10	17	14	10	5	4	6	8	6	8	6	170
B: Nursing intervention	10	2	5	4	5	2	0	4	2	0	0	0	5	3	2	4	1	49
C: Patient action	0	0	0	3	3	0	0	3	0	0	1	0	1	0	0	1	0	12
D: Medical drug- or medical instrument-related	0	0	1	8	3	10	2	3	1	0	2	1	3	1	4	4	2	45
E: Team treatment	6	7	4	10	8	4	5	5	6	6	6	4	2	2	2	5	2	84
F: Medical information management	3	0	0	4	2	3	3	2	6	2	1	3	2	0	4	6	5	46
G: Hospital management	1	0	0	2	2	5	1	3	2	1	2	0	2	1	2	1	0	25
H: Community medicine	0	0	0	1	1	0	0	1	0	0	0	0	2	0	1	1	0	7
I: Medical policy	0	0	0	0	0	0	0	0	0	0	1	0	0	0	0	0	0	1
Total	34	19	20	52	32	38	21	38	31	19	18	12	23	15	21	30	16	439

Source Annexed document Chap. 3: Medical Accidents 2000–16—(conversion from list) by Atsuji Seminar

D: *Medical drug- or medical instrument-related*

Refers to the administration, infusion or preparation of medical drugs including anesthetic preparations for surgery or any other action to support general medical treatment. This includes for example misunderstandings over drug combinations or concentrations and cases where drugs are administered after their expiry date, or where the wrong drug is administered. It also includes mishandling of catheters and other medical instruments supplied by medical manufacturers and defects or flaws in the instruments themselves.

E: *Team treatment*

Refers to secondary medical intervention such as testing, diagnosis and surgical support, including by technical staff (e.g. clinical engineers) auxiliary to surgery, but excluding nursing intervention. This includes for example cases where surgery is carried out based on confusion of test results with those of a different patient and cases where a trainee doctor or someone else other than the staff member responsible undertakes medical intervention with undesired results. Particularly in the advanced medical treatment of today, where it is essential for medical treatment institutions to handle the latest medical instruments and ensure coordination between team members in team treatment, it does not include mistakes by individual staff members but does include mistakes caused by mis-coordination of the medical team.

F: *Medical information management*

Refers to the general range of information management relating to medical systems, including for instance management of patient information, staff shift patterns, and allocation of tasks. This includes for example mis-inputting of electronic records and prescription notes, miscommunication of information between medical profession-als, and misunderstandings over accident information. It also includes injury from side-effects due to multi-drug co-medication or application of different treatment measures in elderly patients consulting multiple medical institutions (there are also cases where confusion arises when patients are prescribed different drugs at a number of different hospitals).

G: *Hospital management*

Refers to governance aspects of national, public and private university hospitals, medical institutions and medical corporations. This includes for example cases of continued long-term use of obsolete technology or long-term re-use of non-re-usable medical instruments, as well as overwork or inadequacies of personnel systems in response to night-time or emergency admissions, regardless of whether at an emer-gency or a regular medical institution.

H: *Community medicine*

Refers to aspects of the coordination of medical institutions and medical corporations with the local community, whether public or private. This includes, for example, cases where communication issues in emergency response lead to delay in arrival of ambulances or buck-passing over emergency patients at the boundaries between the jurisdictions of different prefectural-level authorities.

I: *Medical policy*

Refers to the medical policy and health administration exercised by central government (MHLW) and the healthcare facilities of local government authorities. This includes examples of systemic issues in central government medical policy or other measures, for example the spread of hepatitis B and hepatitis C infection due to a preventive immunization campaign or other measures led by central government.

Regarding the overall trend in the number of accidents, there has been a decreasing tendency since the peak of 52 accidents in 2003. However, it is relevant that, from 2000 to 2016, the factors in medical accidents altered to include not simply medical intervention itself but also team treatment and aspects related to medical drugs and medical instruments (handling) and medical information management (Table 1.2).

The advanced medical treatment of modern times is based on team treatment by a team consisting of a number of medical staff. Faults occurring in this kind of modern clinical setting are discussed by Yamauchi, K. and Yamauchi, T. under the 'snowball model' [13]. If, in a series of medical processes, the first staff member makes a mistake, as long as the second staff member discovers the mistake, the risk of accident will be reduced, but if the mistake remains undiscovered and is perpetuated, the risk of an accident continues to grow. Viewed under this model, the likelihood of the doctors and nurses directly involved with the patient causing an accident will necessarily be heightened, but there will be quite a number of cases where the staff member who makes the final mistake has to bear all the responsibility. If responsibility is not dispersed, individual staff will cover up their own mistakes, and there will be a constantly increasing risk of a further mistake ending up in a medical accident. This is similar to the process in J. Reason's Swiss cheese model [14], in which the route through a series of security holes leads to a major accident.

In team treatment particularly, information sharing on mistakes and near misses and other similar incidents is important, and communication about risks and dangers is essential. In order to use information on medical accidents effectively, we need to see accidents as the result of failures in joint action and very much an issue for medical organizational management systems, rather than pursuing individual responsibility. Incidents and mistakes that have come to light through reporting of medical accidents should be seen as an issue of hospital organizational management rather than of medical professionals and should be treated as an opportunity to remedy inadequacies in medical organizational systems. The utilization of medical accident information is also indispensable from the viewpoint of medical information management, and should not be limited to within the hospital but shared throughout the medical world, helping to construct a 'medical risk management' system to prevent the recurrence of similar situations. Already, in Europe and America, by publishing data on accidents, a system has been introduced for evaluating the reliability of medical institutions. As is the case with aviation accidents, mistakes, to which all are susceptible, are shared, resulting in moves to suppress accidents based on team members learning together and identifying security holes in the wider context.

1.3.2 Co-occurrence Relationship of Accident Causative Factors: Mandala of Failure and Network Mapping

With reference to J. Reason's *Managing the Risks of Organizational Accidents*, we divided the causative factors in modern medical accidents into three levels: direct human factors in the form of human error; system error involving for instance organizational factors leading to accidents and security holes; and background factors that are an indirect breeding ground for above-mentioned accidents (operational management, government policies). The interrelationships between the nine factors are shown in Fig. 1.2.

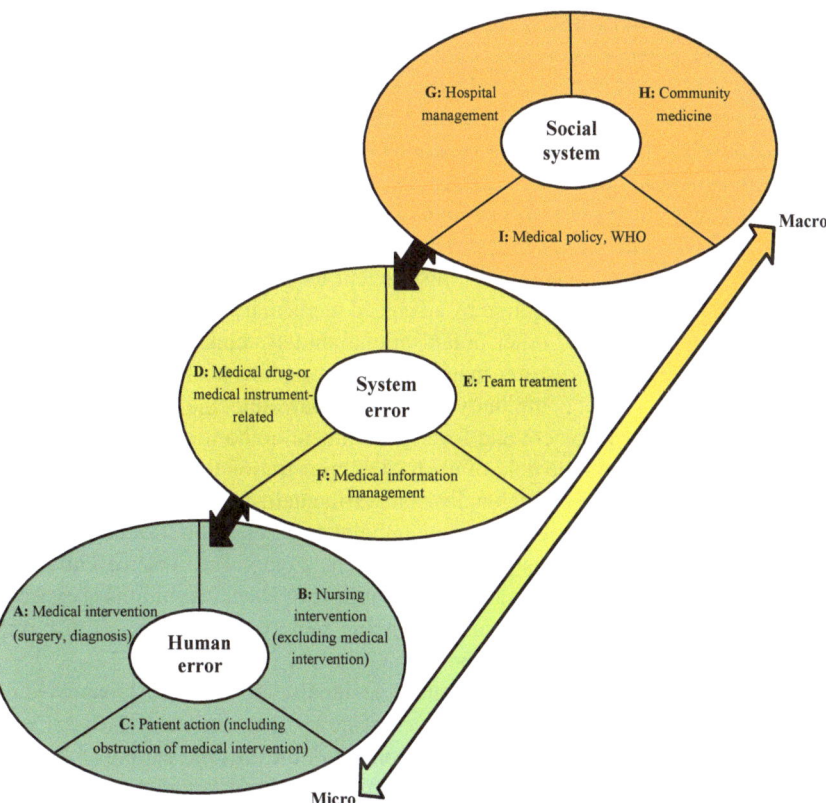

Fig. 1.2 Outline classifications of medical accidents: 3D Mandala of Failure (classification of causes of accident and error). *Note* Drawing by S. Atsuji and R. Fujimoto

In the 3D Mandala of medical accidents, the category of human error includes mistakes during surgery, misadministration of drugs, falls, refusal of treatment and other accident causative factors attributable to issues of technical ability, knowledge, or experience, or to other behaviour on the part of individual doctors or nurses or patients themselves, such as inattention. On the other hand, there are many accidents where the responsibility of the individual medical staff in charge in terms of organizational management is not in question, but where an accident results from a widening of the security holes that lead to error, for instance through inadequate cross-checking within the treatment team, misidentification of drugs with similar names or similar packaging (drug management), mishandling of medical instruments or defects in the instrument itself, or miscommunication or non-sharing of information. Such a situation can be described as system error. In addition to this system error category of medical accident and error, we can also point to issues in hospital management, including human resource management (HRM), such as structural inertia in the hospital organization, mutual learning failure among team members, excessively demanding shift patterns and overwork, failure to invest in medical human resources (lack of opportunity to learn about new advanced medical technologies), and staff stress care.

In addition, complications and other factors increasingly apparent with the aging of society lead to 'multiple external treatment' resulting in side effects due to multiple electronic records and multiple drug prescriptions (this includes cases where the patient seeks a second opinion based on the principle of informed consent and as a result undergoes multiple treatment and unintentionally receives multi-drug co-medication from a number of hospitals, with the patient and the patient's family sometimes losing the ability to manage their own treatment). In addition to such issues with the medical care system, insufficient technical coordination within the treatment team of the kind required by advanced medical treatment, skill imbalances in safety management, and other organizational and systemic factors can be cited as systemic errors where disaster management for medical accident prevention has become essential [15]. In community medicine, meanwhile, the jurisdictional competence of central government and local government authorities presents an issue. Among the issues across the field of medical administration that require review and improvement is the kind of regionally compartmentalized medical administration that leads to buck-passing of emergency ambulance cases and issues in the coordination of emergency hospitals and community medicine. The issue of unforeseen adverse effects from multiple treatments at multiple medical institutions is expected to become increasingly widespread in the aging society, and may result in further additions to the nine factors listed above.

Regarding the concrete details of these accidents, the resource Japan Medical Accident Big Data 2000–16 is a summary of newspaper reports of medical accidents. We used text mining to analyze the content of the articles relating to the accidents listed therein. Fig. 1.3 presents a co-occurrence network map linking accident causative factors to which all people are susceptible.

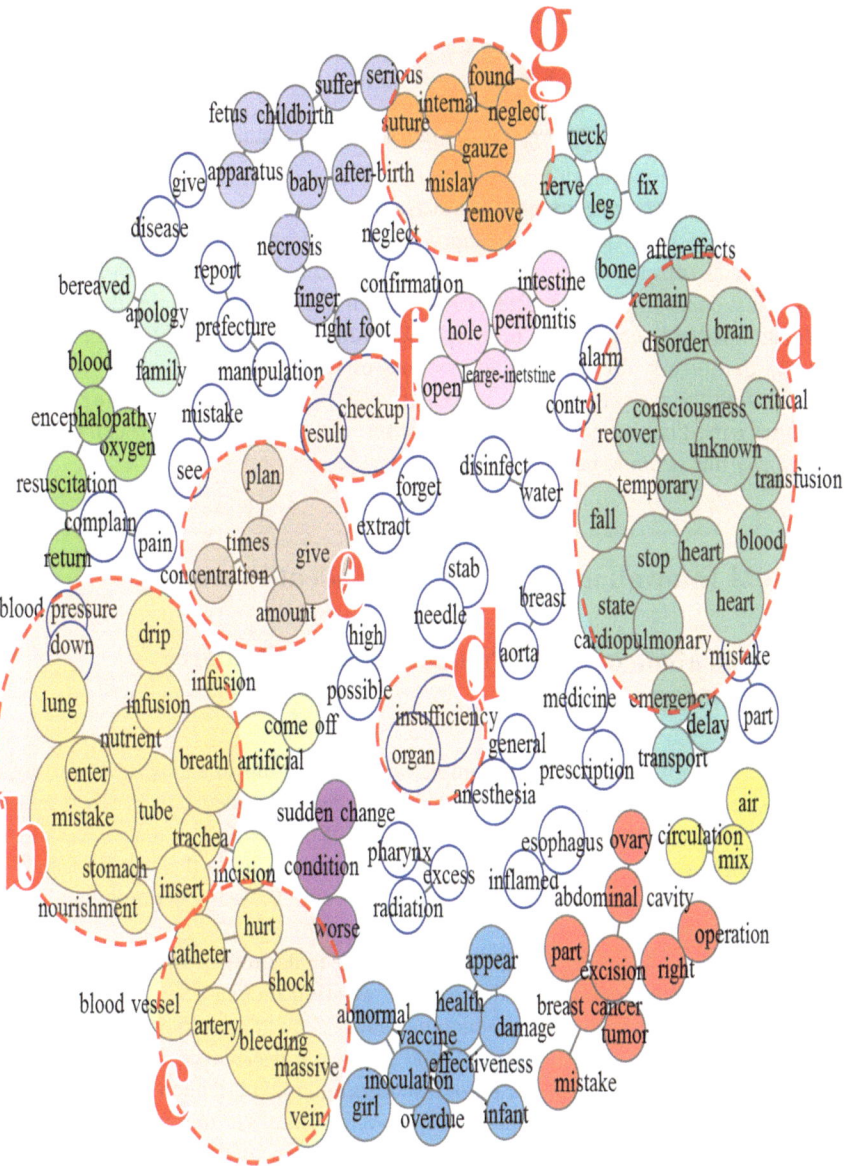

Fig. 1.3 Detailed classifications of medical accidents and errors; newspaper article mapping and cluster classification (the above graph was provided by A. Nozaki based on the big data of Atsuji Seminar). *Note* Co-occurrence network text mining-based visual representation of degree of correlation of accident terminology appearing frequently in newspaper articles (based on text mining of unstructured data on 439 accidents or errors)

Text-mining was carried out on newspaper article data relating to 439 medical accidents in Japan in the period 2000–16, and an analysis made of the degree of correlation of high-frequency terminological items in the articles. The following clusters were identified: (*Group a*) unconscious/condition; (*Group b*) mistake/tube/breathing; (*Group c*) bleeding/high volume; (*Group d*) failure/organ; (*Group e*) administration (drug); (*Group f*) test; (*Group g*) gauze/excision/internal. From these clusters were identified the frequency of high-risk accident patterns. Some of the cluster groups corresponded to elements attracting particular attention in the clinical setting. Other clusters can as a result also be seen as representing checkpoints deserving notice. The treatment in the newspaper articles concentrated on drastic medical accidents of high newsworthiness that grab public attention, but it seems that errors, mistakes, incidents, and misunderstandings tend to move out of focus with the passing of time. In recent years, with a view to reducing medical accidents, a medical support system to overcome accidents of the kind seen in cluster groups *a–g* has become necessary.

1.4 IoM Innovation and Medical Accident Prevention

1.4.1 ICT Medical Innovation and Human Resource Management (HRM)

In the increasingly advanced and complex clinical setting of today, hospital organizations recognize accidents and mistakes as inevitable occurrences. To promote the safety of medical treatment and the creation of confidence, management of the valuable human resources of doctors, nurses, engineers, and other medical staff is an urgent task, and a wide range of related initiatives has already begun in medically advanced nations.

In Europe and America, flight simulators that make use of information on the causes of aircraft accidents shared across the aviation industry are used in training for human resource management, which has led to a sharp reduction in accidents. In medicine similarly, to prevent accidents and errors, it is hoped that the use of medical simulators and other ICT tools for trainee doctors and inexperienced medical personnel could reduce the kind of mistakes that anyone is likely to make. In recent years, the combination of artificial intelligence and robotics has made it possible to acquire technical skills through simulation that reproduces conditions with a high degree of authenticity. Research is also progressing into mixed reality, which combines virtual reality and augmented reality with robotic engineering. If doctors became able to simulate surgery at home using these technologies, this would remove restrictions on medical personnel, who are preoccupied with a host of secondary tasks, and would create opportunities to learn about actual medical intervention and would promote improved technical skills.

Additionally, by using ICT for accident prevention, by using artificial intelligence-supported diagnostic systems to prevent mistakes in diagnosis and prescription, and by sharing accident information through an 'Internet of Medicine' (following IoM) analogous to the IoT, it would be possible to prevent easily occurring misdiagnoses and mis-prescriptions. Further, a fusion of motion capture with robotics could be used to copy the movement techniques of master surgeons, while artificial intelligence could be used to effect 'AI deep learning' of the expertise and knowledge displayed in the diagnosis and prescription practice of veteran doctors. This medical innovation to provide support across the range of medical treatment would be effective in accident prevention. Fig. 1.4 is a graphic representation of the 'hexagonal' medical innovation which this ICT medical technology innovation promises to realize on six fronts. These six fronts correspond to strategies to overcome the medical accident clusters in Groups *a–g* above.

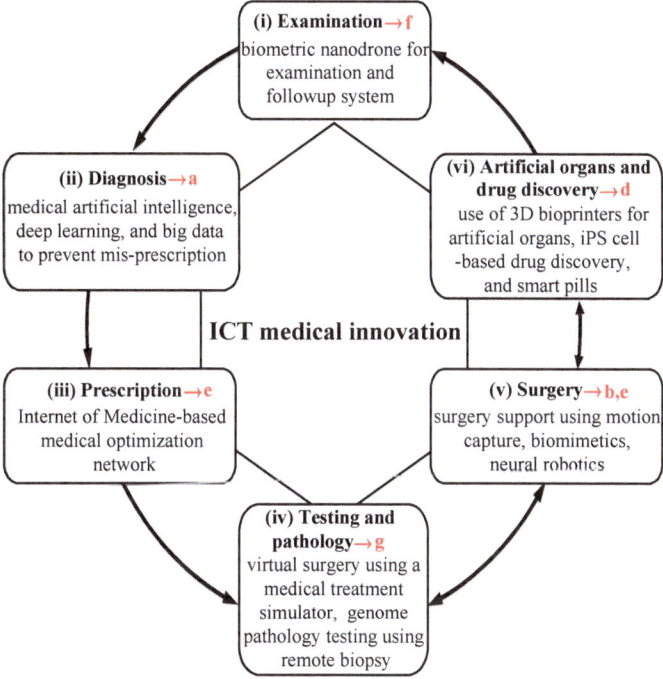

Fig. 1.4 ICT technology applications for medical accident prevention (medical innovation). *Note* Drawing by S. Atsuji and R. Fujimoto

(i) Examination: biometric nanodrone for examination and follow-up system. Imaging of pathological foci within the body using microscopic drones, which are digested and excreted as organic material, to prevent mistakes caused by oversights easily committed in testing. ⇒ Solution for accident prevention in *Group f*

(ii)   Diagnosis: medical artificial intelligence, 'deep learning', and big data to prevent mis-prescription. Use of artificial intelligence for medical diagnosis to explore the range of possible diseases and prevent misdiagnosis. ⇒ Solution for accident prevention in *Group a*

(iii) Prescription: IoM-based medical optimization network. Use of the Internet and big data to gather opinions from a virtual team of medical specialists and prevent diagnosis and prescription mistakes. ⇒ Solution for accident prevention in *Group e*

(iv)   Testing and pathology: virtual surgery using a medical treatment simulator, genome pathology testing using remote biopsy. Use of simulated testing before surgery and prescription to improve technique and instrument handling skills and prevent mistakes in the actual surgery. ⇒ Solution for accident prevention in *Group g*

(v)   Surgery: surgery support using motion capture, biomimetics, neural robotics. To ensure smooth surgical operations, use of robotic technology in areas requiring minute precision to reproduce the movements of experienced surgeons through 'motion capture' and thereby improve surgical precision. ⇒ Solution for accident prevention in *Group b* and *Group c*

(vi)   Artificial organs and drug discovery: use of 3D bioprinters for artificial organs, iPS cell-based drug discovery, and smart pills. Use of biological 3D printers for modeling of patient organs, reproduction of organic organs with 3D bioprinters for use in operations. Also, drug discovery using iPS technology. Smart pills that measure their own effectiveness. ⇒ Solution for accident prevention in *Group d*.

Regarding (iv)–(vi) above, to carry out surgery simulation using an artificial model of the patient organ, the cycle of processes can be reversed or repeated multiple times depending on the circumstances. For prognosis, the cycle returns again to (i).

As part of this ICT innovation, preparations for the use of medical accident big data are currently under way, in connection with which personal information and the scope of its use are issues. When these are resolved and the use of ICT has permeated the clinical environment, it should be possible to realize a platform for real-time sharing on smart medical networks of medical data including accident information.

If not only knowledge of mistakes but also of testing, diagnosis, and prescription were shared, and the enormous amount of data that builds up day by day were used for learning through artificial intelligence this could be expected to help prevent mistakes in all processes and contribute to medical accident prevention. Meanwhile, using the IoT to record and accumulate detailed data on routine items, such as heart rate and number of steps walked, could help put in place a medical support system for the individual patient. If artificial intelligence that learns about individual patient characteristics could be used to automatically prepare medication based on day-to-day physical conditions or provide reminders for clinic appointments, this would also be likely to contribute to avoiding multi-drug co-medication, multiple treatment, or excessive medical consultation. It would also make it possible to allocate limited medical and human resources to the patients who need them most. ICT innovation of this kind could thus be effective in both clinical practice and patient support as a step toward relieving the pressure of work on doctors, nurses, and other medical professionals. In our present research, as a future issue, we are also progressing with investigations into a 'self-learning medical accident database' that uses artificial intelligence gathered from medical accident big data to analyze accident data, classify and arrange by cause of accident, and perform update by learning from accidents.

Of the medical innovations outlined above, experimental application to medical treatment has already begun in the case of artificial intelligence and big data and the IoT. Development is progressing in the use of artificial intelligence to support diagnosis, prescription, etc. The trends in this medical use of ICT are summarized in Table 1.3 Status of ICT use for medical accident prevention.

Table 1.3 Status of ICT use for medical accident prevention

Example of use Name of research institute	Article content (summary)	Source Classification
Nerve regeneration with 3D bioprinter Kyoto University, Cyfuse K.K.	Based on a cluster of cells from human skin, a 3D bioprinter was used to create nerve conduits to successfully regenerate missing nerve tissue. This is expected to lead to treatment methods that cause less physical stress than conventional therapies	Mainichi Shimbun Feb. 24, 2017 (vi) *Group d*
Centralized remote management system for medical instruments Saitama Medical University, Hitachi Systems	Development of a 'centralized remote monitoring system' that notifies medical professionals based on detection of warning signals issued by the various medical instruments used by medical institutions and detection of operating conditions that risk leading to breakdown or irregular operation. It will become possible for the system to centrally collect warning data and operational data from medical instruments made by a range of manufacturers and to check the status of the instruments through smart devices, etc.	Nikkei Shimbun Feb. 7, 2017 (v) *Groups b and e*

(continued)

Table 1.3 (continued)

Example of use Name of research institute	Article content (summary)	Source Classification
Artificial intelligence to save people from blindness Google	Google is developing artificial intelligence able to identify diabetic retinopathy, the main cause of adult blindness. Similarly to artificial intelligence that recognizes faces in photographs or animals, deep learning is used to scan retinal photographs for symptoms. It has been found that artificial intelligence can detect symptoms with roughly the same degree of accuracy as human ophthalmologists	WIRED Feb. 7, 2017 (ii) *Group a*
Optimal cancer treatment guided by artificial intelligence National Cancer Center Japan	Based on scientific papers studying patient cancer gene information and similar clinical data, artificial intelligence proposes optimal anticancer agents and other treatment methods to support doctor diagnosis	Nikkei Shimbun Feb. 1, 2017 (ii) (iii) *Groups a and e*
Informed consent supported by artificial intelligence National Cancer Center Japan	An artificial intelligence system is under development that gauges the degree of patient comprehension in informed consent dialog with a doctor and responds with explanations that include video images	Asahi Shimbun Jan. 31, 2017 (ii) (iii) *Groups a and e*
Artificial intelligence application for early cancer detection with over 99% accuracy Preferred Networks Inc.	Development of technology using deep learning to raise the rate of early breast cancer detection from 80 to 99%. By feeding into artificial intelligence comprehensive analytical data on substances in the blood, genomes, etc., a high rate of accuracy was confirmed in 5000 cases. Testing of improved safety and much higher accuracy will reportedly become possible with only a very small blood sample. Application is expected to several dozen different types of cancer	Nikkei Shimbun Jan. 28, 2017 (ii) *Group a*

(continued)

Table 1.3 (continued)

Example of use Name of research institute	Article content (summary)	Source Classification
Instant clinical judgment with artificial intelligence based on symptoms and test values Jichi Medical University	System developed which responds to input of patient symptoms with artificial intelligence-based proposal of a number of differential diagnoses and calculation of the probability of each. When medical information on new patients is recorded in artificial intelligence which has assimilated scientific papers and textbooks containing information on the sensitivity and specificity of the differential diagnoses, it responds by displaying the most likely diseases, their probability, the test items required for differential diagnosis, and the names of drugs prescribed to patients diagnosed in the past with the same disease	Nikkei Medical Jan. 16, 2017 (ii) (iii) *Groups a and e*
IoT drug calendar Kobe University	In outpatient treatment, including home-based medical care, to identify the accuracy of patient drug compliance, a drug compliance management system has been developed. The system provides four pockets for each day, one each for morning, midday, after the evening meal, and before bedtime, and records data on when and from which pocket the drug was taken. Analysis of the data is used to identify the appropriate amount of drug and to provide guidance on drug compliance	Nikkei Shimbun Jan. 13, 2017 (v) *Groups b and e*
Augmented reality to support surgery Tokyo Women's Medical University, Intel	Development of a system is in progress which will use CT data, etc., to allow surgeons to carry out indirect manipulation through intuitive hand movements, without touching any implements, to indicate where to make an incision or which position to rotate to for optimal view. Advantages of allowing operation with one hand and maintaining sterile conditions	JB Press Dec. 20, 2016 (v) *Groups b and e*

(continued)

Table 1.3 (continued)

Example of use Name of research institute	Article content (summary)	Source Classification
Artificial intelligence to explore treatment methods Kyoto University, Fujitsu	Artificial intelligence development is in progress which will deduce the cause of patient disease from genetic information and will explore individually tailored treatment methods. Artificial intelligence will learn from a database of worldwide medical scientific papers, genome data, etc. In addition, the system aims to clarify the relationship to disease of gene mutations whose pathological significance is not yet clear	Asahi Shimbun Oct, 6, 2016 (ii) *Group a*
Start of trials of high blood pressure treatment via remote medical examination Tokyo Women's Medical University	Trials have started to test the safety of IoT-based remote treatment for patients with high blood pressure. Patients will manage data on home-based blood pressure measurements using a dedicated app, which the attending physician checks regularly to decide on treatment policy. Consultation takes place by videophone, online chat, etc., followed by drug prescription. Drugs are prescribed in hospital and are sent to the patient's home	Mainichi Shimbun Sept. 14, 2016 (iv) *Group g*
Theater-type operating space Japan Agency for Medical Research and Development Tokyo Women's Medical University Hiroshima University	IoT is used to create a linked network throughout the operating theatre to integrate basic data on medical instruments, intraoperative imaging, the position of surgical instruments, the patient's physical condition, etc. Integrated tracking of the progress of the operation and patient condition improves the accuracy and safety of treatment by allowing surgical navigation and the movement of instruments to be monitored. The varied information collected during surgery is converted to database format and used to support improved treatment	Nikkei Shimbun July 4, 2016 (v) *Groups b and e*

(continued)

Table 1.3 (continued)

Example of use Name of research institute	Article content (summary)	Source Classification
Computer graphics-based virtual surgery practice Kyoto University	A system is under development to reproduce organs on a personal computer to allow various trial procedures ahead of surgery, for instance the exploration of a range of surgical approaches. The doctor moves a cursor that looks like an electrical surgical knife to manipulate and dissect the computer graphic liver, which changes shape in response, calculating and displaying the resulting change in the position of blood vessels and tumors	Yomiuri Shimbun Oct. 12, 2015 (v) *Groups b and e*

Note Surveillance by R. Fujimoto and S. Atsuji

As of February 2017, a wide range of systems has been developed, from support for medical examination and diagnosis using artificial intelligence and big data to surgical support and simulation based on augmented reality and IoT-based centralized management of medical instruments. Trials aimed at practical realization are under way. Going forward, innovative medical treatment is anticipated in four areas: artificial intelligence-supported diagnosis; medical motion capture; medical accident big data; and 3D bioprinters. There are also experimental initiatives to expand patient support and remote medical treatment, raising the task of flexible system design for ICT utilization.

We are now entering an age when 'medical treatment democracy' will be an issue. For Japan, which is experiencing the aging of its population at a rate unparalleled elsewhere in the world, this requires a revision of medical treatment policy. The falling birth rate is also contributing to a change in the nation's age structure, making it clear that enhanced policy making is required in the area of medical treatment as well as in long-term care, pensions, insurance, and welfare. Across the media, each day brings new reports of a variety of new medical treatment technologies and special treatment methods. At the same time, meals, facilities and the other amenities of inpatient institutions and other factors such as employment conditions for hospital staff have become relevant points in the patient's selection of hospital. However, it is self-evident that the foundation of the quality of medical treatment is safety. It is this core competence of medical treatment—patient safety—that should be the main focus for medical professionals.

1.4.2 Compliance and Governance Exemplified in a 'Medical Sustainability'

As exemplified in the medical intervention at a university hospital presented in the case study below, team treatment is at the center of modern medical treatment, with an increasingly complex range of operations and procedures requiring coordination between doctors, nurses, and clinical engineers. Particularly in the treatment of intractable diseases, new medical technology is increasingly sophisticated, conventional knowledge is inadequate by itself, and division of tasks through auxiliary medical technology adds to the complexity. Likewise, in the medical accident presented in the example below, knowledge of the artificial heart-lung machine not being correctly transmitted from the engineer to the doctor was one of the causes of the accident. So that increasingly complex medical teams can continue to function, communication skills that enable timely treatment decisions are essential. Medical teams are supported not only in the immediate surgical environment, but also by a variety of testing technologies and computer engineers, making communication within the team ever more important. If this exchange of meanings is inadequate, a frequent result is malfunction of the team treatment. Communication failures involve concurrent appearance of human error and system error.

Human error is inevitable as all people are liable to make mistakes, and accidents can happen even in highly skilled medical teams. Of course, medical professionals pay the closest attention in the discharge of their medical duties, but there has been no decrease in the number of medical accidents and errors. In the past, the focus in medical accidents was on individual human error, while the underlying system error tended to remain out of focus. The present book closes in on the security holes that cause the system error that in turn underlies human error. Up till now, medical treatment institutions, as a preventive measure against accidents, have tended to highlight the responsibility not of systemic arrangements but rather of human personnel, issuing penalties such as pay cuts, demotion, and dismissal depending on the number and seriousness of mistakes as part of a system of guaranteeing medical safety through personnel management. As a result, however, in order to avoid penalties for accidents, medical personnel protect each other in the event of mistakes or failures, creating a culture of self-protecting complicity in concealment, which has not brought a decrease in accidents. This inappropriate medical treatment management has not been brought to public attention so there has been no reform of safety management in hospital organizations and the same types of accident have been repeated. In the clinical environment, diagnostic mistakes, surgical mistakes, drug prescription and administration mistakes, patient misidentification, mistakes in patient handover and many other types of accident occur at the frontline. In order to avoid these kinds of accident and secondary disasters, experience and knowledge of failures must be organizationally harnessed for hospital system safety management through 'double-loop learning' (March, J. G. and Argyris C.) practised mutually among the members of the organization.

According to Yamauchi, K. and Yamauchi, T., 'Japanese university medical departments, which are rated highly for their research and practical achievement but not for their education, have a structure which makes it difficult for professors and other senior doctors to be enthusiastic about the training of junior doctors or the treatment of patients not involved in research projects' [16]. University hospitals, reportedly, have an ingrained system which places emphasis on research performance and results. Meanwhile, university hospitals are divided internally into chairs and departments, so that 'the independence of each medical unit is strong, making it is difficult for the hospital as a whole to agree on new systems for accident prevention or to take sweeping measures' [17]. Of course universities must respect the independence and originality of research, but to improve medical safety, organizational management and systemic frameworks must be put in place to allow their effective functioning as medical treatment institutions for the patient's benefit.

In the case study below, for fear that the accident would be made public and the hospital's failure leak to the outside, a medical accident was covered up and the information kept sealed within the organization. The internal culture of the hospital had created a self-protecting approach of safeguarding the professional position of staff members, which blocked the appropriate response to the accident, which is to inform the patient or the bereaved family. In the future, as an anti-disaster initiative also serving to reduce medical accidents, it is time to additionally consider the reform of governance functions in medical organizations.

In the event of a medical accident, medical personnel experience a range of mental burdens, which can lead to psychological trauma. In the deep psychology of medical personnel, an opposition arises between the code of the hospital organization and the doctor's individual codes, and the accident becomes the occasion for a conflict to emerge between the doctor's personality and the organization personality as a member of the hospital staff. The conflict of codes between the code of the hospital organization as a medical treatment institution and the medical professional's codes emerges at the same time as the medical accident, and is latent during the period of mistake-free medical intervention. Together with the acknowledgment of accidents and failures, there emerges an imbalance between the dual claims of medical codes and organizational (hospital staff) membership, and the evasion of this contradiction becomes normalized, tending to continuously strengthen the organizational affiliation [18], so that thinking patterns become centered on the organization personality. In the continued existence of any organization, 'the fiction of superior authority is generated, and authority is reproduced within the everyday routine of organizational participation' [19]. Medical personnel, in addition to their individual personality and organization personality, have the social personality aspect of their medical personality, and are thus burdened with a three-layered persona.

In the case study below of an accident cover-up attempted by doctors, the strict hierarchical relations within the workplace and the emphasis on performance determined by the hospital organizational culture, worked, following the occurrence of the accident, to destroy the balance between the doctors' personess, which had been in equilibrium. In the internal psychology of doctors who had adopted an organization personality, the obedience to and desire for authority and the overemphasis on performance among other factors seem to have led to a loss of morality and a susceptibility to panic. In reaction to the authoritarian culture and absolute hierarchy which gave rise to the accident, governance with functions to remedy these issues may be worthy of consideration as a new social function to prevent medical accidents reaching disaster scale.

In general, medical accident cover-ups are carried out in order to protect society's trust in the hospital and the status of the doctor. They thus constitute activity to guarantee the authority of medical treatment as a whole. On the other hand, they also contain aspects which infringe against patient confidence in medical treatment and against legal compliance. If medical accidents are repeated, they cause social unease and loss of confidence in medical treatment. The case study below examines a classic example of internal reporting of a medical accident at a university hospital. According to Barnard, 'Organizations endure, however, in proportion to the breadth of the morality by which they are governed' [20]. For the advancement of medical treatment, the creation of a morality that maintains compliance can be seen as an essential professional competence of the managers of the hospital organization. This is only to say that foresight, long purpose, and high ideals are the basis for the persistence of beneficial cooperative relationships within the hospital organization.

As seen in the case study, silencing and cover-up of mistakes means losing forever the opportunity to learn from accidents. Mutual learning from accidents may also be an experience allowing improvement of the quality of medical treatment. Generally, medical staff during their lifetime will on many occasions have faced the death of a patient and the grief of the bereaved family, and will therefore be carrying a burden of conflict and trauma. In a profession which confronts directly the harsh realities of human life, these opposing aspects can wear down the demanding 'moral codes' required as the ethics of medical workers and lead to the antisocial actions of falsification of records and cover-up, and this could be the fate of anyone. To prevent accident cover-up, it is necessary to lighten the responsibility of doctors by allocating responsibility for accidents to the organization as a whole. What is needed is a systemic and managerial reform that safeguards the position of those involved in the accident, thus making it easier to gather accident information and review the failed actions. This would promote overall medical safety by allowing the sharing of accident information.

Going forward, improving levels of safety will no doubt result from the 'democratization of medical treatment' now under way in medically advanced overseas nations, following the recognition of the need to promote medical safety by making accidents public on the responsibility of the medical treatment organization and to promote mutual learning and sharing of insights into failure prevention. There are few reports of medical accidents from developing countries, but the more medically advanced a nation, the greater the number of accident reports, because the resulting reform measures are shared across the whole of society. Instead of concealing accidents, it is important rather to discover the security holes that mediate accidents. Today, thanks to the enactment of the Whistle blower Protection Act, which gives legal protection against unfair treatment to insiders who make reports, and thanks also to the amendment of the Medical Service Law, the number of accidents made public is increasing. In 2015, the number of accidents reported to the Japan Council for Quality Health Care, at 3654 cases, was approximately three times greater than ten years earlier [21]. It should be noted that already, in the United States, as in the aviation industry, responsibility for the occurrence of accidents is not attributed to individuals (doctors or pilots); rather, through disclosure and identification of the security hole that led to the accident, the organization as a whole and the industry as a whole shoulder the responsibility, leading to improvement of the overall system.

References

1. Eunjung, C. A., "Researchers: Medical errors now third leading cause of death in United States", *The Washington Post*, May 3, 2016.
2. Leape, L. L., "Errors in Medicine", *JAMA*, December 21, 1994-Vol 272, No. 23, pp. 1851–1857.
3. Reason, J., *The Human Contribution: Unsafe Acts, Accidents, and Heroic Recoveries*, Ashgate Publishing, 2008.
4. Brennan, T. A., Leape, L. L. and Laird, N. M., "Incidence of adverse events and negligence in hospitalized patients: Results of the Harvard Medical Practice Study I", *The New England Journal of Medicine*, 324: 370–376, 1991.
5. Kohn, L. T., Corrigan, J. M. and Donaldson, M. S. (eds.), *To Err is Human: Building a Safer Health System Committee on Quality of Health Care in America: Institute of Medicine*, National Academy Press, 1999.
6. Donaldson, L., *An Organization with a Memory: Report of an Expert Group on Learning from Adverse Events in the NHS Chaired by the Chief Medical Officer*, National Health Service, The Stationery Office, 2000.
7. Japan Medical Association (edi.), *Iryōjūjisha no tame no iryō anzen taisaku manyuaru.* (*Manual of medical safety measures for medical professionals*), 2007.
8. Leape, L. L., Brennan, T. A. and Laird, N. M., et al., "The nature of adverse events and negligence in hospitalized patients: Results of the Harvard Medical Practice Study II", *The New England Journal of Medicine*, 324: 377–384, 1991.
9. Hilfiker, D., "Making medical mistakes: How doctors harm patients-and themselves", *Harper's Magazine*, Harper's 34, 1984.
10. Sexton, J. B., Thomas, E. J. and Helmreich, R. L., "Error, Stress, and Teamwork in Medicine and Aviation: Cross-sectional Surveys", *BMJ*, 320: 745–749, 2000.
11. Simon, R., Salisbury, M. and Wagner, G., "MedTeam: Teamwork advances emergency department effectiveness and reduces medical errors", *Ambul Outreach*, Spring, 21–4, 2000.
12. Reason, J., *Managing the Risks of Organizational Accidents*, Ashgate Publishing, 1997. (Translated by Shiomi H., Takano K., Sasō K., *Soshiki jiko: okorubekushite okoru jiko kara no dasshutsu*, JUSE Press, 2001, p. 173).
13. Yamauchi, K. and Yamauchi, T., *Iryō jiko* (*Medical accidents*), Asahi Shimbun Company, 2000, p. 102.
14. Reason, J., *op. cit.*, 1997, pp. 16–17.
15. Atsuji, S., *Unsafety: Disaster Management, Organizational Accidents, and Crisis Sciences for Sustainability*, Springer, 2016.
16. Yamauchi, K. and Yamauchi, T., *op. cit.*, p. 206.
17. *Ibid.*, p. 206.
18. Sasaki, T. (edi), *Gendai keieigaku no kihon mondai*, (Basic problems of modern business management science), Bunshindo, 1999, p. 213.

19. Simon, H. A., *Administrative behavior: A study of decision-making processes in administrative organizations,* Macmillan Publishing, 1945 (3rd edition, The Free Press, 1976).
20. Barnard, C. I., *The Functions of the Executive*, Harvard University Press, 1938, pp. 282–283.
21. Japan Council for Quality Health Care, *Iryō jiko jōhō shūshū tō jigyō heisei 27-nendonenhō*, (*Medical accident data collection and other projects*), Annual Report, 2015.

Chapter 2
A Case Study of Medical Accidents and Errors for *Kaizen*

2.1 Case Study of a 2001 Medical Accident

Publicity, newspapers on March 2, 2001, a medical accident occurred in the pediatric cardiology department of a university hospital. The case involved an accident caused by a surgical team under the charge of Dr. A during a heart operation on a 12-year-old patient. The accident occurred despite the hospital being known as the institution with Japan's leading level of technology in the field of cardiac surgery. Below is presented the timeline of the accident (as featured in the *Asahi Shimbun*) (Table 2.1).

In the heart surgery performed in this case, after bringing the patient's heartbeat to a complete halt, a small sternotomy is performed. Before the commencement of surgery, a procedure is carried out in which the patient's heart is temporarily stopped and blood drained from the body and reintroduced to circulation after oxygenation. The operation of the artificial heart-lung machine which takes over the functions of these organs was assigned to Dr. B.

When using a heart-lung machine, first of all a procedure known as gravity drainage is applied. However, as the drainage operation was not sufficiently effective, Dr. B switched part of the way through from gravity drainage to vacuum-assisted venous drainage in an attempt to correct the insufficiency. Then, following an instruction from Dr. A to secure visibility at the surgical site, Dr. B raised the speed of the blood suction pump to almost three times the regulation value. As a result, the patient's blood circulation became insufficient, causing the patient to suffer severe brain damage. A medical accident thus took place due to errors in the operation of the artificial heart-lung machine. Newspapers on March 5, three days after surgery, the patient died.

© The Author(s), under exclusive license to Springer Nature Singapore Pte Ltd. 2019
S. Atsuji, *Resilience Management for a Sustainable Aging Society*,
SpringerBriefs in Business, https://doi.org/10.1007/978-981-13-5805-0_2

Table 2.1 Typical case study of medical accident

2001	March 2	Patient undergoes heart surgery at a university hospital
	March 5	Patient dies of cerebrovascular failure. Dr. A instructs staff including chief nurse to falsify intensive care unit records
	March 8	Dr. A instructs clinical engineers to falsify records of artificial heart-lung machine
		Document claiming errors in operation of artificial heart-lung machine and falsification of records is delivered to university management
	March 9	Letter with same content is delivered to patient's father
		Head professor of Dr. A's department reports to hospital director that no accident has taken place
	May 25	Patient's father requests hospital to undertake inquiry into artificial heart-lung machine and related factors
	June 21	Hospital sets up committee to investigate cause of death
	October 3	Committee presents report recognizing errors and cover-up through falsification of records
	December 8	Two doctors visit patient's father and make apology
	December 29	Errors in surgery and cover-up are revealed, hospital director apologizes at press conference
2002	January 8	Patient's father reports six doctors and other staff members to Tokyo Metropolitan Police Department on suspicion of causing death by professional negligence
	January 9	MHLW and Tokyo metropolitan authorities undertake on-site investigation at hospital
	February 18	Hospital reaches out-of-court settlement with parents on condition of measures to prevent recurrence and other conditions
	June 28	Drs. A and B arrested by Tokyo Metropolitan Police Department
		Hospital holds press conference and announces abandonment of status as advanced treatment hospital and voluntary withdrawal from heart transplants
	July 12	MHLW decides to withdraw designation as advanced treatment hospital

Source Asahi Shimbun; Surveillance by S. Atsuji

2.2   Cover-up of the Medical Accident and Emergence of Internal Allegation

The bereaved family was not told by the hospital that the cause of death was a medical accident caused by erroneous operation of the artificial heart-lung machine. The fact of the error was known only to the members of the surgical team and a small number of hospital officials. However, Newspapers on March 8, three days after the patient's death, the hospital's chief administrator received an anonymous report from within the hospital claiming that the cause of the patient's death was brain damage due to a medical accident and alleging further that falsification of the surgical record had taken place at the chief instigation of Dr. A, who had been in charge of the surgical team. According to the allegation, following a direct instruction from Dr. A with the aim of covering up the medical accident, the chief nurse and other staff had altered an entry on the first page of the intensive care unit record so that instead of the original pupillary dilation value of 7 mm it now showed a value of 4 mm. From the second page of the record onward, Dr. A himself, using the same method as on the first page, had falsified 13 entries to conceal the medical accident.

Newspapers on March 3, the day after the operation, Dr. B and the clinical engineer, having received orders from Dr. A, amended the recorded dosage of a drug used to treat brain damage, which had been administered in excessive amounts, to show the normal dosage. They also altered the figures for the patient's body temperature. It was the engineer who had made the original entry whom Dr. A first instructed to falsify the artificial heart-lung machine record, but as this engineer was absent due to being a trainee on secondment from another hospital, the two-page record was in the end falsified as instructed by an engineer from within the hospital. Publicity, newspapers on March 9, the hospital responded to the allegations with an order from the hospital's chief administrator to the head professor of the department to undertake an investigation and establish the facts of the matter.

The family of the deceased patient received a similar note. This marked a decisive turning point for the family, who included medical personnel and who had already become suspicious on seeing the patient after the operation because of her lack of pupillary response. On May 25, the bereaved family, who felt mistrustful of the reports received from the hospital, requested that the hospital undertake an investigation into the facts of the operation. So, more than three and a half months after the accident, the hospital set up an accident investigation committee to undertake a full-scale inquiry.

Seven months after the operation, on October 3, the accident investigation committee set up by the hospital presented a report recognizing that a medical accident had taken place. The report contained statements accepting that Dr. A and other staff had falsified records in an attempt to cover up. However, it also stated that the hospital as a whole had not been involved in the cover-up. On January 8, 2002, the bereaved family took the step of raising a complaint against the doctors involved and on June 28, Drs. A and B were arrested by the Tokyo Metropolitan Police Department. In response to this case, the hospital maintained that the doctors had acted on the basis of independent judgment and that the hospital was not guilty of negligence. The question of the hospital's criminal responsibility was indeed never raised, and the hospital director and the head professor of the department stepped down on reaching retirement age at the end of March 2001.

2.3 Mechanism of Medical Accident Occurrence

In his work *Managing the Risks of Organizational Accidents*, James Reason presents the Swiss cheese model. With reference to this model, in our analysis of medical accidents as represented by the present case, which occurred at a university hospital, we examined the causative factors using an analytical framework consisting of: (I) safety-specific factors, (II) procedural factors, (III) medical technology factors, and (IV) management factors (Table 2.2).

Table 2.2 Mechanisms of medical accident occurrence in the case study

(I) Safety-specific factors	*Safety measures, emergency resources and procedural manuals, safety outside work, etc.*	
	Inadequate provision of manuals	In the vicinity of the blood drainage tube, there were no notices or manuals warning of excessive pump speed and other risks or indicating that insufficient blood drainage could result from rise in pressure. If these had been provided, the accident could have been prevented and appropriate measures been taken to counter the blood drainage insufficiency. It would also have been a routine encouragement to staff to ensure understanding of medical instrument systems. At the time of the accident, the team panicked and was unable to respond calmly. To prevent this kind of situation, the provision of simple warning notices and manuals might well be effective
	Absence of clinical engineers	In the pediatric cardiology department, doctors operated the artificial heart-lung machine in rotation. However, compared to engineers specializing in such machines, the doctors had insufficient understanding of the system due to inexperience and the difficulty of keeping up with technological advances. During regular operation, this lack of knowledge was not problematic, but in the event of an accident, it was manifest as an inferior ability to respond, which was bound to have a crucial effect on the therapeutic outcome. Thus, in the present case, none of the doctors was able to identify the cause of the blood drainage insufficiency or to take appropriate countermeasures, whereas the engineer who was sent for did take appropriate action. For the doctor, who tends to be concentrating attention on the operation itself and whose priority is the condition of the patient, it is difficult to maintain focused operation of such a device. Its operation should therefore have been assigned to an engineer and the necessary number of engineers should have been provided. If the device is nevertheless operated by a doctor, adequate technological training is required. However, the pediatric cardiology department provided no training whatsoever

(continued)

Table 2.2   (continued)

(II) Medical procedural factors	*Operational procedures, supervisory control, equipment operational procedures, professional regulations, etc.*	
	Misoperation of blood suction pump	The reason for the excessive speed applied to the suction pump was that Dr. B had not been aware of the risk of rising pressure in the device, which is a disadvantage of vacuum-assisted venous drainage. For this reason, Dr. B complied with Dr. A's instruction to raise pump speed without misgivings
	Doctor's misconception	During the initial phase of the operation, altering the position of the drainage tube relieved the blood drainage insufficiency. It was also conceivable that the suction force at the tip of the blood drainage tube could cause blockage by acting on the vascular wall. The surgical team moreover had previously noticed that the blood drainage tube was liable to become bent at an unnatural angle. Because of this combination of factors, Dr. B became convinced that the cause of the blood drainage insufficiency lay in the mispositioning of the drainage tube, and did not consider other possibilities
	Insufficient understanding of instrument system	The medical team lacked correct knowledge of the mechanism of vacuum-assisted venous drainage. They were therefore not in a position to understand the risk of excess speed in the suction pump and condensation on the filter causing pressure to rise in the device and leading to blood drainage insufficiency. The clinical engineer who rushed to assist immediately took action to relieve the pressure, which resolved the technical problem. This indicates clearly that, if only proper understanding of the system had been present, appropriate judgment and response would have been possible
(III) Medical technical factors	*Technically controlled devices, design, hardware, etc..*	
	Missing stop valve	The reason for the patient suffering brain damage was to a great extent connected with the fact that the internal pressure of the reservoir became positive. In the general use of the vacuum-assisted drainage method, the risk of such a situation arising was widely recognized. It is also clear from statements made by experts in the Medical Safety Management Committee that this risk is recorded in the literature. If a valve to prevent positive pressure had been fitted, it is likely that the system would have been rendered safe and the change to positive internal pressure could have been prevented. At other medical treatment institutions, the fitting of a device to prevent positive pressure was carried out. But the pediatric cardiology department did not apply this measure on a comprehensive basis

(continued)

Table 2.2 (continued)

	Lack of monitoring device	To react to the danger of rising internal pressure in the device, equipment to monitor pressure is required. In the present case, the blood drainage circuit was fitted instead with a vascular wall negative pressure monitor. However, there was a filter between the reservoir and the monitor, and if this filter was even partly closed, internal pressure could not be measured, meaning that this replacement was not appropriate
(IV) Hospital management factors	*Communication, system management, leadership ability, operational management, etc.*	
	One-way communication	When asked by the external investigative committee whether Dr. B's switch to vacuum-assisted venous drainage had been communicated to the whole medical team, the doctors and other staff present said that it had not. It is clear that communication between the team operating the artificial heart-lung machine and the team undertaking the surgery did not flow smoothly. There was a strict hierarchical structure within the department which meant a one-way connection between the two teams, resulting in failure to communicate meaning successfully. Moreover, the relationship between the doctors was one of unconditional obedience. These factors meant that Dr. B obeyed Dr. A's order to raise the speed of the suction pump in order to secure visibility at the surgical site. There was thus nothing to stand in the way of excess speed being applied to the suction pump
	Authoritarian relationships	The head professor of the department placed a disproportionate emphasis on performance-based results. Moreover, given the leadership style that brooked no opposition from junior staff, there was an authoritarian structure which maintained a hierarchy with the departmental professor at its apex. From the perspective of nurses and engineers, the doctor's word was absolute, and there was no room for even expressing an opinion to the doctor in what became a one-way relationship. Because of this, the engineer's information and knowledge of the risks inherent in vacuum-assisted venous drainage could not be shared with the doctor. When an incident occurred, the latter was thus unable to take appropriate action

In addition to procedural errors in medical interventions, defective operation of medical instruments, and factors relating to the hospital's systems, the causes of the medical disaster included the practices and conventions of the wider medical world and its implicit authoritarian character. These are graphically represented in Fig. 2.1.

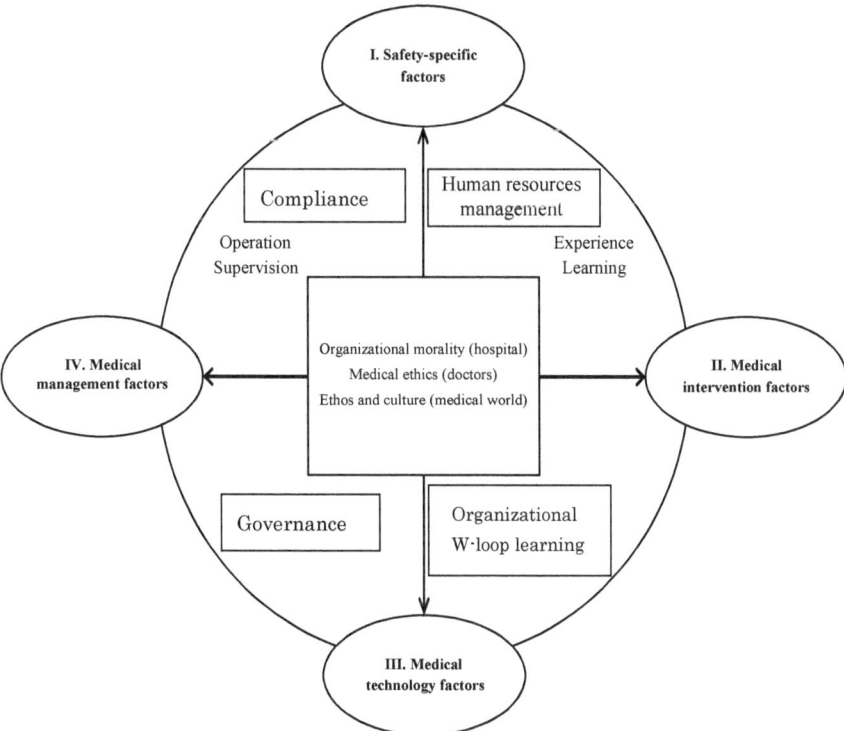

Fig. 2.1 Mechanism of occurrence of medical accidents. *Source* J. Reason *Managing the Risks of Organizational Accidents*, Union of Japanese Scientists and Engineers, 1999, based on pp. 172–173

In the present case, in addition to the above issues, there were also problems in the personality of the individual doctor's ethics and the morality of the hospital. Before the operation, there was a dispute between Dr. A and the victim's father (a dental surgeon) regarding the way the surgery had been explained. So, after the operation, because he thought that a complaint would be raised if the medical accident were to come to light, Dr. A did not report the facts of the brain damage. Thus, the desire to avoid a worsening of his reputation as team leader led him to issue the order for the cover-up. In a statement after his arrest, it was revealed that the motivation for the medical file falsification was that he feared a worsening of his professional reputation as a doctor and sought to avoid this through concealment.

Since the establishment of a pediatric cardiology department in the cardiovascular surgery department of the hospital's cardiac research center, a situation had arisen whereby interference from other departments was not tolerated. This gave free rein to the department head professor's damaging leadership approach of giving absolute priority to performance-based results, and medical treatment became removed from the perspective of patient and societal needs. This led ultimately to the creation of a departmental climate in which even the falsification of medical records was accepted if required to cover up an accident. The nursing and anesthesia departments belonged to the overall hospital organization and functioned as part of it; thus, despite the fact that its staff had been ordered to undertake the falsification of medical records by a doctor, the director of the nursing department ducked the responsibility of the position by failing to take action. The doctors from the anesthesia department involved in the operation were aware of the fact that the brain damage was due to error. As the hospital had failed to put in place an adequate structure for reporting medical accidents, It seems reasonable to point to an organizational culture that bred structural inertia and had led to a secretive approach and learning disability throughout the hospital.

2.4 Future Issues: Interorganizational Relations and Structural Inertia in Japanese Medicine

Japanese medicine is supervised and administered by central government and the MHLW and operates a medical insurance system unique in world terms, which is highly regarded by other nations for its universal healthcare coverage and other advantages. However, there are issues with related organizations, such as the Japan Pension Service. As part of Japan's scarcely credible system of arrangements, there was a postwar industrial support strategy worked out between government and private enterprise which extended into areas of the social state such as public health, medical treatment, welfare, pensions, and long-term care. Within the historical context of postwar reconstruction, policies to support industry had the result that the prescription records of the national population, which should normally be managed by the state, are accessible to private life insurance firms and the life insurance industry through life insurance industry cooperatives and the network of regional national health insurance organizations, thus giving these firms direct insight into the medical history of members of the public. This collusive relationship between the state and private enterprise is a specifically Japanese system which, from the viewpoint of personal information and data security, should have no place in a modern society. It is a setup incomprehensible to other countries.

Through the auxiliary network of National Health Insurance Organizations, which carries out central control of patient medical record prescription receipts, the mutual life insurance cooperatives, which are cooperatives of private-sector life insurance companies, carry out effective processing of the nation's prescription receipts. As a result, it is said that patients with cancer insurance, due to a system for specifying the date of confirmed cancer diagnosis, without which cancer insurance is not available.

The stakeholders of medical treatment are first and foremost patients (citizens), but doctors and nurses and clinical engineers are of course also included, and the category also extends to medical treatment institutions (operation) and managerial and supervisory government offices and administrative organs. Meanwhile, there are various research organizations and therapeutic and surgical approaches, and the various institutions have their own distinct therapeutic and surgical approaches and associated terminology and nomenclature, etc. Medical treatment institutions thus have a highly diversified range of distinct expertise but this medical world with its history and tradition is likely to undergo standardization in the future.

2.5 Conclusion: Potential for a Global Database Based on Medical Accident Big Data

① The view that ICT should be used in the clinical setting was reflected in interviews with only a number of doctors; in order to raise the accuracy of surgery, advance simulations would be useful in which the necessary patient organ models (including blood vessels and nerves) are reproduced using a 3D bioprinter, which would reduce costs and preparation time.

② To cover the sequence of medical procedures—testing → diagnosis → prescription → surgery → post-surgery, etc.—(team treatment), it would be useful to develop a network system for artificial intelligence-based diagnostic analysis to check for oversights in test results and provide diagnostic support. Before surgery, it would be beneficial to use motion capture or other technologies to record the protocol in a medical simulation of the surgical procedure, allowing doctors to practice at home on a personal computer.

③ Regarding medical accidents, which are the present subject, sharing of big data worldwide is essential in order to avoid repeating the same accidents and errors. Compared to America and Britain, Japanese medical accidents frequently involve the same failure points and similar accident scenarios.

④ There are many similarities for instance in the misoperation of similar medical instruments. Sharing of medical accident big data through a global database, with mutual worldwide disclosure of accidents wherever they happen, might work in the future to intercept unfortunate accidents in advance. To take full advantage of the opportunity presented by big data based on the numerous accident reports from medically advanced nations, it would be effective for accident prevention to assemble big data on medical accidents into a global database. Medically advanced nations can of course point out the possibility of concealment and falsification to cover up medical accidents. In Japan, accident reports are very few and the probability of a medical accident being reported is abnormally low compared to the medically advanced nations of Europe and North America, as pointed out by L. Leape. So can Japan be called a medically advanced nation? As well as fulfilling the plea from patients and medical personnel not to let the same mistakes and accidents be repeated, perhaps the democratization of medicine in this country requires the more extreme step of international comparison based on a global database?

Chapter 3
Evidence: Medical Accidents Drowing from Big-Data 2000–2016

The medical accidents and negligence reported frequently in the medically advanced nations of the United States, United Kingdom, and Japan are widely claimed to have been due not only to 'human error' but also to 'system error' within the medical management process in hospital organizations. Using ill-structured big-data on actual examples of medical accidents and negligence in the 17 years from 2000 to 2016, the present study analyzed more than 430 medical accidents reported in the pages of newspapers in Japan. The study adopts the following structure: first part, diversibility of medical accidents reported by newspapers with big-data; second part, the causative factors are classified from nine different perspectives using ill-structured big-data on the 439 medical accidents to visualize a 'failure Mandara'; and third part, Japan Council for Quality Healthcare tackled with the bibliography of medical accident and healthcare treatment. Rather than criticizing medical staff, hospital organizations and government policy, the aim of the study is to achieve an improvement (*Kaizen*) in medical care services in the near future for next age. The socialization of medical accidents is a feature of medically advanced nations, accompanying the democratization of medical treatment. On the other hand, in countries with less developed medical treatment systems, there is a tendency for medical accidents not to be publicized.

3.1 Medical Accidents Categories in Japan

The definition of big data varies from field to field, but generally refers to a data set within a given time series that is in standard format but massive in scale, or which is in non-standard format and unstructured. The present paper deals with unstructured text data in non-standard format consisting of newspaper articles on medical accidents covering the 17-year period from 2000 to 2016 (439 incidents) and I have therefore used the term 'big data' (see: Ministry of Internal Affairs and Communications: Information and Communications White Paper, 2012 Edition).

© The Author(s), under exclusive license to Springer Nature Singapore Pte Ltd. 2019   37
S. Atsuji, *Resilience Management for a Sustainable Aging Society*,
SpringerBriefs in Business, https://doi.org/10.1007/978-981-13-5805-0_3

Table 3.1 Medical accident categories in Japan

Japan, the Ministry of Health, Labour and Welfare and the Japan Medical Association

(i) **Medical accidents and medical errors**

Medical accident is a comprehensive term which includes all case of personal injury arising at any stage in the medical treatment process at a location connected with medical treatment, whereas medical error refers to a case where patient injury results from a medical professional neglecting to exercise due care in the medical treatment process

(ii) **Incident**

Refers to a situation in the routine course of medical practice where the patient does not sustain injury, but a near miss or close call is experienced

(iii) **Error**

A human action is classified as an error for instance where (1) it is not intended by the agent (2) it is undesirable with reference to regulations (3) it is undesirable from the viewpoint of a third party (4) it fails to satisfy objectively expected standards

(iv) **Misunderstanding**

Misunderstanding is a form of error in which something not actually present is thought to exist or something present is not correctly identified. This may for instance be the mishearing of verbal communication, misreading of written information or displays, misreading of data on instrumentation, misunderstanding in an accustomed operation, or misidentification of a patient. This may be the cause of a medical accident

Note Indicates that, in Japan, medical accident is the main term used in a wider sense, while medical error appears to be used in a narrower sense. In Europe and North America, medical accident categories are different: firstly, a distinction is made depending on whether the medical intervention results in adverse effect on the patient and secondly a distinction is made between preventable and unpreventable events depending on whether negligence is present. The present book adopts a definition of medical accident and error in accordance with the classification of the MHLW, but it is likely in future that the categorization of medical accidents will move toward an international standard

In Japan, accident prevention initiatives were launched in response to a medical accident in 2001, of which we will make a case study later. In 2002, the MHLW and the Japan Medical Association published accident prevention guidelines (Table 3.1).

In Chap. 4 below, Medical Accidents and Errors 2000–2016, the cause of the accidents in the data list is classified in accordance with MHLW criteria on medical accidents, errors, incidents, and misunderstandings. However, there is a tendency in recent years for incidents to occur frequently that do not fit into the existing categories, and I have therefore attempted a reclassification based on assignment to at least nine causative factors. Table 3.2 presents the results of text mining of year-by-year unstructured data in non-standard format arranged by these accident causes.

Table 3.2 (In detail above-mentioned Table 1.2) 2000–16 Statistical trend in medical accidents by cause of accident

	2000	2001	2002	2003	2004	2005	2006	2007	2008	2009	2010	2011	2012	2013	2014	2015	2016	Total
A: Medical intervention	14	10	10	20	8	14	10	17	14	10	5	4	6	8	6	8	6	170
B: Nursing intervention	10	2	5	4	5	2	0	4	2	0	0	0	5	3	2	4	1	49
C: Patient action	0	0	0	3	3	0	0	3	0	0	1	0	1	0	0	1	0	12
D: Medical drug- or medical instrument-related	0	0	1	8	3	10	2	3	1	0	2	1	3	1	4	4	2	45
E: Team treatment	6	7	4	10	8	4	5	5	6	6	6	4	2	2	2	5	2	84
F: Medical information management	3	0	0	4	2	3	3	2	6	2	1	3	2	0	4	6	5	46
G: Hospital management	1	0	0	2	2	5	1	3	2	1	2	0	2	1	2	1	0	25
H: Community medicine	0	0	0	1	1	0	0	1	0	0	0	0	2	0	1	1	0	7
I: Medical policy	0	0	0	0	0	0	0	0	0	0	1	0	0	0	0	0	0	1
Total	34	19	20	52	32	38	21	38	31	19	18	12	23	15	21	30	16	439

Source Annexed document Part II: Medical Accidents 2000–16 (conversion from list)

Regarding the trend in the total number of accidents, after a peak of 52 in 2003, there has been a decreasing tendency. From 2000 to 2016, however, *it is apparent that the causative factors in medical accidents changed from factors related to medical intervention itself to factors related to team treatment, medical drugs instruments (and their operation),and medical information management.* With reference to J. Reason's *Managing the Risks of Organizational Accidents,* I have classified these contemporary medical accident factors into three levels: the direct anthropogenic factor of human error; system error such as organizational factors and security holes that underlie the occurrence of accidents; and background factors (management/policy) present in the indirect environment of the accident (Fig. 3.1). The mutual interconnections of the nine factors are shown in 3D Mandala of Failure of Medical Accidents.

As shown in Fig. 3.2: 3D Mandala of medical accidents, surgical mistakes and drug misadministration, falls and refusal of treatment and other accident factors deriving from failures of technical ability, knowledge, experience, attention, etc., on the part of individual doctors, nurses or patients themselves are taken to be human error. Human error also includes many accidents for which responsibility cannot be attributed to the individual medical staff in charge, such as inadequate cross-checking within the treatment team, misidentification of drugs with similar names or similar packaging (drug management), and miscommunication or non-sharing of information. These are vulnerable 'security holes' and factors that open them wider so that an accident results can be classed as system error. The scope of system error as a form of medical accident and error covers issues in hospital management, including human resources management (HRM), such as excessively demanding shift patterns and overwork, failure to invest in medical human resources (lack of opportunity to learn about new advanced medical technologies), and staff stress care; the issue of 'multiple outpatient treatment' among elderly patients with complicating illnesses, a problem of aging societies with falling birth rates, which results in multiple electronic records and multiple drug prescriptions (this includes cases where the patient seeks a second opinion based on the principle of informed consent and undergoes multiple treatment, with the result sometimes that the patient and the patient's family lose the ability to manage their own treatment); and organizational system error such as insufficient technical coordination within the treatment team of the kind required by advanced medical treatment and skill imbalances in safety management. A response in terms of modern disaster management is essential. In addition to the examples above, the scope of system error also includes systemic issues such as the regionally compartmentalized medical administration that leads to buck-passing of emergency ambulance cases, and issues in the coordination of emergency hospitals and community medicine.

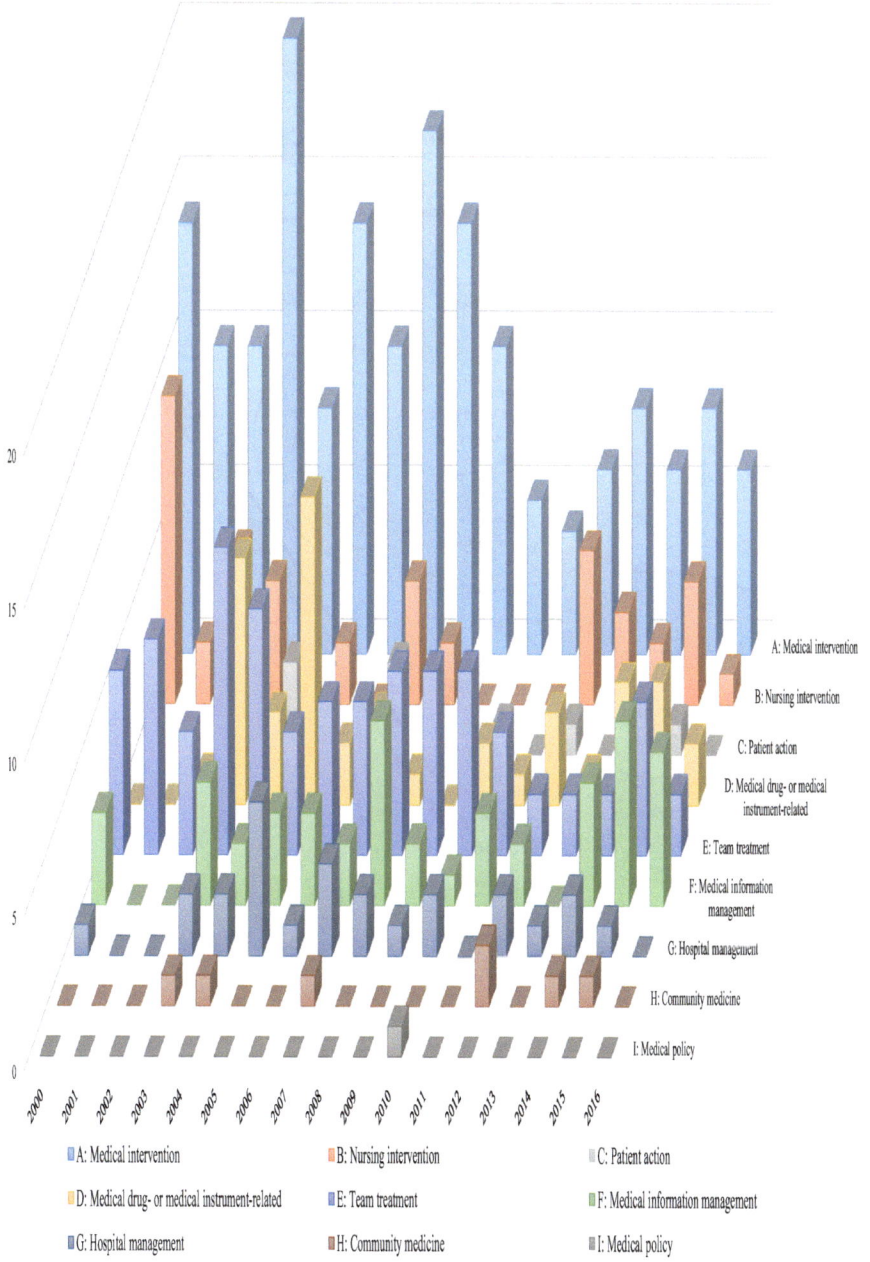

Fig. 3.1 (In detail above-mentioned Fig. 1.1) Intermediate classification of medical accidents: trend in number of events by cause (Japan, 2000–16). *Source* Medical Accidents 2000–16: Statistical Trends by Cause of Accident (3D graphic representation using above Table 3.2)

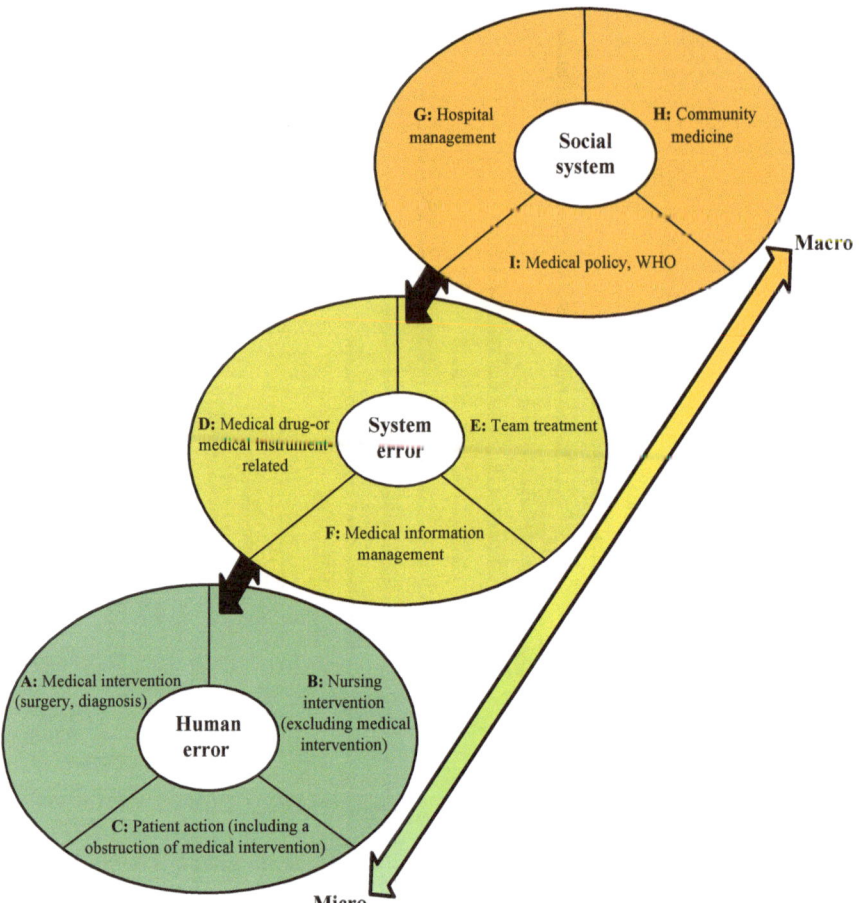

Fig. 3.2 (In detail above-mentioned Fig. 1.2) Outline classification of medical accidents: 3D Mandala of Failure (classification of causes of accident and error)

Regarding the specific details of these accidents, Part II of the present document, Medical Accidents and Errors 2000–2016, presents a summary of the medical accidents reported in the press. The newspaper articles presented in chronological order in the accident list were subjected to analysis based on text mining. The degree of correlation among frequently appearing terms is presented in Fig. 3.3: Co-occurrence Network Mapping.

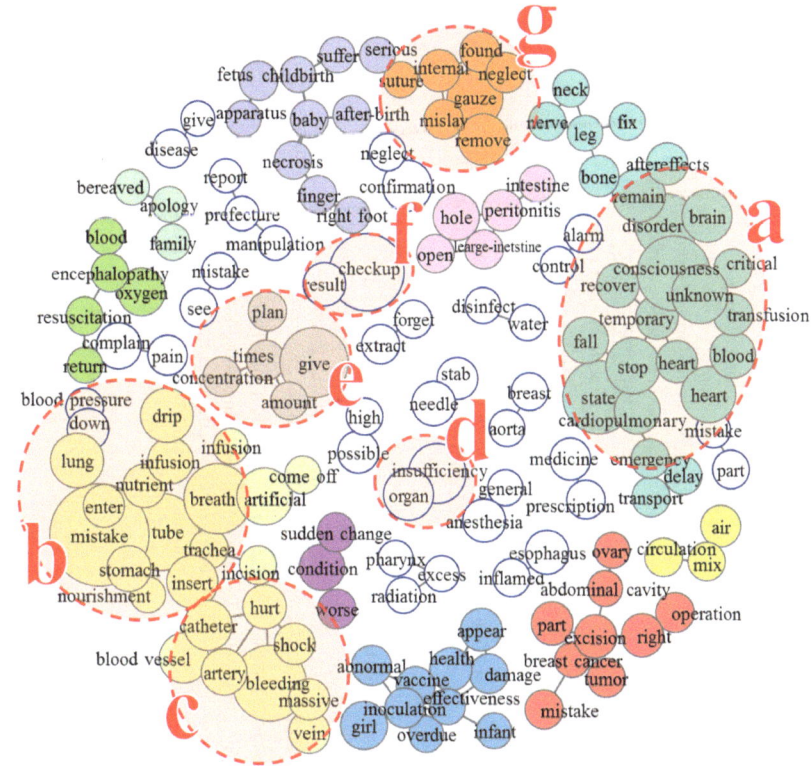

Fig. 3.3 (In detail above-mentioned Fig. 1.3) Detailed classification of medical accidents and errors; newspaper article mapping and cluster classification (the above graph was provided by A. Nozaki based on big data by Atsuji Seminar). *Note* Co-occurrence network text mining-based visual representation of degree of correlation of accident terminology appearing frequently in newspaper articles (based on text mining of unstructured data on 439 accidents or errors)

3.2 Medical Accidents and Errors 2012–2016 (in Detail)

Newspaper article publicity on 439 data Japanese medical accidents in the period 2000–2016 were subjected to text mining and the degree of correlation among terms appearing with high frequency in the articles was analyzed. The following general clusters were identified (a) unconscious/condition; (b) mistake/tube/breathing; (c) bleeding/high volume; (d) failure/organ; (e) administration (drug); (f) test; (g) gauze/excision/internal. From these clusters was identified the frequency of 'high-risk accident patterns'. Meanwhile, each cluster corresponded to elements requiring particular and constant attention in the clinical setting, and can be seen as a checkpoint associated with high risk of medical accidents. The treatment in the newspaper articles concentrated on drastic medical accidents of high newsworthiness that grab public attention but errors, mistakes, incidents, and misunderstandings seem to move out of focus with the passing of time (Table 3.3).

Table 3.3 Medical accidents and errors 2012–2016 (in detail)

Date	Accident or error Name of medical institution	Injury or harm	Content of newspaper article (extract)	Source Classification
2012 Mar. 1	Patient suffered sequelae due to inattention during post-surgical observation Ashiya Municipal Hospital	Female in 70s suffered sequelae in left leg	Due to inattention during clinical observation after arthroplasty for left thigh fracture, sequelae in the form of paralysis of the left leg. Female nurse failed to check the condition of a surgical strap	Asahi B
2012 Mar. 22	Bladder surgery mistake resulted in death of male patient in 80s Mutsu General Hospital	Male in 80s died due to perforation of bladder	During surgery to remove bladder tumor, doctor's mistake caused bladder perforation resulting in death	Asahi A
2012 Apr. 20	Mistake during resuscitation leaves patient in serious condition with risk of lasting brain damage Osaka City University Hospital	Female in 40s left with risk of permanent brain damage	Mistake in assembly of resuscitation bag supplying oxygen to lung caused hypoxic encephalopathy in leukemia inpatient with risk of lasting brain damage	Mainichi G
2012 June 8	Doctor misread test results, cancer became aggravated Niigata Prefectural Koide Hospital (currently Koide Hospital)	Aggravation of esophageal cancer in male in 60s	Esophageal cancer became aggravated after mistaken explanation of test results. Despite the esophageal cancer being at an early stage, no treatment was given due to mistaken test results	Asahi F
2012 June 20	Mistake during living-donor liver transplant resulted in necrosis of toes of infant Kumamoto University Hospital	Tip of infant's big toe fell into necrotic state	Drip infusate leaked into tissues outside blood vessels during living-donor liver transplant operation and tip of big toe fell into necrotic state. Calcium chloride is thought to have been the possible cause of the necrosis	Mainichi A

(continued)

Table 3.3 (continued)

Date	Accident or error / Name of medical institution	Injury or harm	Content of newspaper article (extract)	Source / Classification
2012 June 20	Female patient died after feeling unwell after a stomach cancer screening at Higashiomi City / Higashiomi City, Shiga Prefecture	Death of female in 50s	Complained of feeling unwell after a stomach cancer screening in which a foaming agent and barium were given before X-ray. After the screening, the patient collapsed in the waiting room of the mobile screening unit and died after being transferred to hospital	Mainichi / H
2012 July 12	Mistaken drug administration to patient led to temporary reduced consciousness / Hyogo Prefectural Awaji Hospital	Female in 80s developed serious shock symptoms due to allergy	Different inpatient's medication was mistakenly administered. Following a failure to check the patient's name, the female inpatient was given drip infusion of a penicillin drug intended for another patient	Asahi / B
2012 Aug. 1	Nurse mistakenly cut respirator tube. / Hospital apologized / Takarazuka City Hospital	Female in 50s died of multi-organ failure	Report of medical accident in which part of inpatient's artificial respirator tube was mistakenly cut with scissors by nurse. The female patient died on the 13th of multi-organ failure	Mainichi / B
2012 Aug. 2	Male patient suffered stroke after failure to expel air from drip infusion bag / Osaka City General Hospital	Male in 60s survived but with possible paralysis of right side of body	Female nurse forgot to expel air from infusion bag, leading to stroke due to air entering the patient's cerebral blood vessels	Mainichi / B

(continued)

Table 3.3 (continued)

Date	Accident or error Name of medical institution	Injury or harm	Content of newspaper article (extract)	Source Classification
2012 Aug. 23	Stomach and inserted tube mistakenly sewn together in surgery Kita-Kyushu Municipal Medical Center	Male in 60s. No sequelae	Medical accident in which tube inserted during stomach surgery was mistakenly included in suture. When joining the stomach and small intestine, the surgeon inadvertently also passed the stitch through the tip of the tube used to drain the stomach contents	Mainichi A
2012 Aug. 31	Medical mitten tore, leading to amputation of necrotized finger Kobe City Medical Center West Hospital	Necrosis of forefinger of female in 70s	Medical mitten tore and thread became wrapped around finger of inpatient, leading to necrosis and amputation. The patient, who had brain dysfunction and was admitted for a disease of the internal organs, had a medical mitten put on her right hand after she pulled out an indwelling tube	Asahi C
2012 Sept. 18	Respirator shut down, possibly because nurse forgot to switch electric power on National Center of Neurology and Psychiatry	Death of female in 30s	Muscular dystrophy patient died. After procedure to drain phlegm from patient, staff forgot to switch the artificial respirator on	Mainichi B
2012 Sept. 26	Mistake in assembly of respiratory support equipment during emergency resulted in death of two patients. Alert issued by Japan Council for Quality Health Care	Death of two patients	Two cases of patient resuscitation being hindered by mistake in assembly of manually operated respiratory support equipment used in emergencies. After assembling the respiratory support equipment, staff did not check its proper functioning	Mainichi G

(continued)

Table 3.3 (continued)

Date	Accident or error / Name of medical institution	Injury or harm	Content of newspaper article (extract)	Source / Classification
2012 Oct. 1	Hemostatic agent mistakenly injected instead of anesthetic during surgery, leading to temporary loss of consciousness Shinshu University Hospital	Male in 80s lost consciousness temporarily	Hemostatic agent was injected during surgery instead of anesthetic. Nurse asked by doctor for anesthetic mistakenly handed over the hemostatic agent, which the doctor injected	Mainichi D
2012 Nov. 1	Gauze left in nose for 19 years Mito Medical Center	Male patient. Subsequent development unknown	Medical gauze left for 19 years in back of nose of male patient after surgery. Patient underwent nose-related surgery at the former Mito Hospital. Was examined at a different hospital due to severe pain, where a remnant of the gauze was found	Mainichi E
2012 Nov. 7	Male child inoculated with influenza vaccine instead of inactivated polio Pediatric medical institution in Nagasaki Prefecture	17-month old male. No damage to health	Mother asked for influenza vaccine for herself, and preventive inoculation with inactivated polio vaccine for her son, but the influenza vaccine was mistakenly given to the child	Mainichi D
2012 Nov. 15	Inoculation with expired vaccine Hospital in Uki City	12-year-old male. No damage to health	Expired measles-rubella vaccine mistakenly inoculated at a city hospital. The hospital had failed to carry out checks before inoculation, resulting in the use of vaccine one week past its expiry date	Mainichi D

(continued)

Table 3.3 (continued)

Date	Accident or error Name of medical institution	Injury or harm	Content of newspaper article (extract)	Source Classification
2012 Dec. 1	Male died when ambulance was mistakenly sent to patient at different address with same name Yokohama City Fire Control Command Center	Male in 60s died after cardiopulmonary arrest	Due to mistaken instruction from the municipal Fire Control Command Center, the ambulance was sent to a patient at a different address with the same name as the patient in his 60s who rang the ambulance after feeling unwell. The ambulance arrived with a delay of around 30 min, by which time the patient was in a state of cardiopulmonary arrest	Mainichi H
2012 Dec. 1	Lasting damage when patient was not given instruction to take or restart normal medication Aki General Hospital	Patient left with severe damage	Patient was left with severe damage. Patient had been taking normal medication but was told to discontinue despite no test being carried out. On the discharge sheet, the doctor did not mention the discontinuation and the patient did not restart administration	Asahi F
2012 Dec. 12	Severe brain damage arising from mistake in heart surgery Nagoya City University Hospital	Female in 60s left with severe brain damage	Attachment of blood supply tube was inappropriate leading to severe brain damage in female patient. Tube supplying blood from heart-lung machine was inserted too deep into the cardiac aorta resulting in insufficient bloodflow to the brain	Mainichi A
2012 Dec. 14	Gauze left behind in patient undergoing surgery Osaka City Juso Hospital	Male in 30s. No sequelae	Sheet of gauze was left behind in body of patient undergoing surgery to remove part of colon. The operation was conducted by a male surgeon. Gauze sheet was found in X-ray on rear side of colon	Asahi A

(continued)

Table 3.3 (continued)

Date	Accident or error / Name of medical institution	Injury or harm	Content of newspaper article (extract)	Source / Classification
2012 Dec. 18	Stem cells were transplanted to different female child due to mistaken identity National Center for Child Health and Development	4-year-old female No damage to health	Hematopoietic stem cells harvested from a 1-year-old male to be reimplanted in the same patient were mistakenly transplanted to a 4-year-old female. Thought to be a case of patient misidentification. Transplant to female patient in neighboring room with same disease	Mainichi E
2012 Dec.	Tube left behind in patient's body Kobe City Medical Center General Hospital	Foreign object in body of male in 60s, removed. No sequelae	When male patient had surgery for back pain, a tube for draining collected blood out of the body was sewn in together with the surgical wound suture	Mainichi A
2013 Jan. 1	Kidney donor died 34 days later. Reported to the relevant academic society Saitama Medical University International Medical Center	Death of male in 60s	Male donor in a living-donor kidney transplant died 34 days after surgery. Thought to have developed severe pneumonia	Mainichi G
2013 Jan. 31	Gauze left in body for 18 years after surgery Former Kochi Prefectural Sukumo Hospital (currently Kochi Prefectural Hata Kenmin Hospital)	No damage to health	Gauze left inside a female patient's body for around 18 years. An operation to remove the gauze was carried out and there are no related health issues. A shadow thought to indicate the gauze was found during a test for a separate disease	Asahi A

(continued)

Table 3.3 (continued)

Date	Accident or error / Name of medical institution	Injury or harm	Content of newspaper article (extract)	Source / Classification
2013 Feb. 7	Infant suffered burn during treatment, resulting in toe amputation / Hospital in Hadano City, Kanagawa Prefecture	Infant suffered burn and had toe amputated	Male child with breathing difficulties and hypothermia suffered burns on the toes of both feet during hospital treatment, resulting in amputation. The child developed breathing difficulties after drinking breastmilk or other substance, but was not brought straight to hospital and therefore became hypothermic	Mainichi / E
2013 Apr. 1	Male in 50s died after duodenal surgery / Gunma University Hospital	Death of male in 50s	Patient death around 11 months after duodenal surgery. Patient underwent surgery to remove a duodenal tumor. The procedure was switched to laparotomy and the tumor was resected. After the surgery, however, the patient developed liver dysfunction and died of liver failure	Mainichi / A
2013 Apr. 30	Patient death following high-concentration acetic acid administration / Yokohama City University Hospital	Death of female in 50s	Death of female who received administration of high-concentration acetic acid solution. Nurse administered 18 cc acetic acid solution with doctor's permission. Patient recovered temporarily but suffered cardiac arrest and died the following day	Mainichi / E
2013 May 1	Gauze left in body after surgery / Sagamihara Chuo Hospital	Female in 30s. No sequelae	Surgical gauze was left behind in abdomen of female patient undergoing laparotomy for acute appendicitis. Laparotomy was performed for suspected peritonitis, during which the appendix and pus were removed	Asahi / A

(continued)

Table 3.3 (continued)

Date	Accident or error Name of medical institution	Injury or harm	Content of newspaper article (extract)	Source Classification
2013 May 13	Patient died of blood loss during surgery Nagasaki City Public Hospital (currently Nagaski Harbor Medical Center)	Death of male in 70s from severe hemorrhage	Male in 70s died of severe hemorrhage following injury to right pulmonary artery. During cancer resection, as a tube was being inserted from the exterior to join with another blood vessel, the right pulmonary artery was damaged by a surgical instrument, leading to uncontrolled bleeding	Asahi A
2013 May 20	Foreign object left behind in body after surgery Okitama Public General Hospital	Female in 50s, measures and procedures necessary	One year after abdominal surgery, female patient had a CT scan as part of regular testing, in which a foreign object was found in the abdominal cavity	Mainichi A
2013 May 24	Mistaken resection of part of an organ Kanazawa Medical University Hospital	Male in 30s mistakenly suffered resection of part of the pancreas	Part of the pancreas was mistakenly removed. During endolaparoscopy, a tumor was removed from the left adrenal gland of a male patient. On investigation of the resected organ after the operation, it was found that part of the pancreas had also been removed	Asahi A
2013 Aug. 1	A needle intended to be placed in a vein on the left side of the neck was mistakenly inserted in the artery Kitasato University Hospital	Patient in 60s died of multi-organ failure	Needle intended to be placed in a vein on the left side of the neck was mistakenly inserted in the artery, causing an excessive dose of anticoagulant agent. The patient suffered a severe hemorrhage on the right side of the neck, resulting in compression of the airway. The patient subsequently died of multi-organ failure	Mainichi D

(continued)

Table 3.3 (continued)

Date	Accident or error Name of medical institution	Injury or harm	Content of newspaper article (extract)	Source Classification
2013 Aug. 22	Infant received mistaken administration of antibiotics at 10 times required concentration leading to necrosis of toes Hyogo Prefectural Kobe Children's Hospital	A 1-month-old infant suffered necrosis of three toes on right foot	Mistaken administration of antibiotics at 10 times the regulation concentration caused necrosis and amputation of 3 toes on the right foot. A female nurse diluted the antibiotics with water for infusion and the doctor administered it by infusion above the heel	Mainichi B
2013 Aug. 27	Male patient died after air entered the pulmonary vein during surgery Minoh City Hospital	Death of male in 70s	Male patient died during lung cancer surgery following mistaken introduction of air into the pulmonary vein	Mainichi A
2013 Oct. 13	Death of inpatient after staff fail to notice alarm sound of electrocardiogram for around 10 min Saiseikai Kawaguchi General Hospital	Death of female in 70s	Despite activation of alarm of electrocardiogram monitor, nurses failed to notice and female patient died	Mainichi B
2013 Nov. 6	Medical tape blocked the tracheal stoma of a patient, causing death by asphyxiation Ehime Prefectural Central Hospital	Death of male in 70s	Former nurse caused death of male patient by blocking a tracheal stoma in the throat with non-air-permeable medical tape	Mainichi B
2013 Nov. 26	Death due to failure to detect lung cancer Municipal Tsuruga Hospital	Death of male in 80s	Male patient died due to lung cancer being overlooked. Patient was examined after collapsing at home and died after metastatic brain tumor was found on CT scan. The patient had undergone chest X-ray as a dialysis patient	Mainichi A

(continued)

Table 3.3 (continued)

Date	Accident or error Name of medical institution	Injury or harm	Content of newspaper article (extract)	Source Classification
2014 Feb. 18	Male child died. Bereaved family had received 'no explanation of sedative drug' Tokyo Women's Medical University Hospital	Death of 2-year old male child	Death following administration of sedative contra-indicated in children. Family claim that no prior explanation was given that sedative was to be used and that dose was excessive, demanded apology and clarification from hospital	Mainichi F
2014 Mar. 1	Damage to spinal cord during erdoscopic surgery Kitakyushu Municipal Medical Center	Male in 40s left with sequelae including motor impairment	During endoscopic surgery for intervertebral hernia, damage occurred to the spinal cord. The patient was left with sequelae including motor impairment. A male doctor in his 40s was in charge of the surgery. The surgery was to reduce a bone that was compressing the spinal cord	Mainichi A
2014 Apr. 1	Mistaken administration of contrast medium Center Hospital of the National Center for Global Health and Medicine	Death of female in 70s	During spinal cord imaging investigation where the contrast medium isovist for spinal cord imaging should have been used, urografin 60% injection fluid was mistakenly used instead. The female patient's condition deteriorated suddenly and she died	Mainichi D
2014 Apr. 25	Transfusion of wrong blood type led to aggravation of symptoms and death of neonate Kanagawa Children's Medical Center	Death of neonate aged 28 days or less	Neonate was given transfusion of platelet fluid of wrong blood type, leading to deterioration of condition and death. When giving transfusion of blood type A platelet fluid, a syringe from another patient containing type O platelet fluid was attached to the transfusion pump	Asahi F

(continued)

Table 3.3 (continued)

Date	Accident or error Name of medical institution	Injury or harm	Content of newspaper article (extract)	Source Classification
2014 Apr. 28	Patient suffered nerve damage and sight loss in left eye due to surgical error Nagasaki University Hospital	Data not published on patient request. Sight loss in left eye	During surgery to remove polyp from paranasal cavity accidental damage to the optical nerve caused sight loss in left eye. As the endoscope was being inserted into the nose to access the polyp, damage was accidentally done to the nerves of the left eye	Mainichi A
2014 May 19	Prohibited re-use of surgical instrument Kinki-chuo Chest Medical Center	Around 2300 patients	Surgical instruments used in thoracoscopy and whose re-use is prohibited were re-used over a period of 6 years from May 2008 up to April 2014	Mainichi G
2014 May 23	Patient death after delayed ambulance arrival due to mistake in locating address Iida Regional Fire Department Headquarters	Death of male in 70s	Ambulance arrival at patient's home was delayed by 10 min after emergency 119 call. Male in 70s who had complained of headache and abdominal pain died at the hospital. Investigation initiated into the role played by the delay	Mainichi H
2014 June 1	Death of lung cancer patient due to insufficient information sharing. Apology by hospital Nagoya University Hospital	Death of male in 50s	Despite signs of lung cancer on computed tomography, it was overlooked due to information not being shared between doctors, and the male patient died two years later	Mainichi F

(continued)

Table 3.3 (continued)

Date	Accident or error Name of medical institution	Injury or harm	Content of newspaper article (extract)	Source Classification
2014 June 17	Mistake in collection of sample during breast cancer screening, breast resected in unnecessary surgery Takasago Municipal Hospital	Female had part of her breast removed	It was established that the sample had been confused with that of another breast cancer patient. The female patient had only a benign tumor in her breast, but was misdiagnosed with cancer, and had unnecessary surgery in another hospital in which part of her breast was removed	Mainichi E
2014 July 1	Lack of coordination within hospital prevented accurate diagnosis Takaoka City Hospital	Death of male in 50s from Brugada syndrome	Incomplete data in electronic medical records and lack of coordination within hospital meant that the cardiovascular tests required for accurate diagnosis were not carried out and the patient died	Mainichi F
2014 July 22	Mistake in catheter insertion resulted in cardiac arrest and unconsciousness Osaka City University Hospital	Female in 60s unconscious in serious condition	During change of catheter it was mistakenly inserted outside the blood vessel, and as infusion continued, the female patient suffered temporary cardiac arrest and remained unconscious after resuscitation. The catheter was changed and found not to have been inserted into the blood vessel	Mainichi A
2014 Aug. 1	Gauze left behind in surgery to remove brain tumor Kobe City Medical Center General Hospital	Female in 40s made full recovery	150 gauze sheets were used in the partial resection of a brain tumor. An abscess was suspected at the surgical site and confirmation was carried out. On the same day, it was discovered in surgery that one sheet of gauze had been left behind	Mainichi A

(continued)

Table 3.3 (continued)

Date	Accident or error Name of medical institution	Injury or harm	Content of newspaper article (extract)	Source Classification
2014 Aug. 20	Female patient died after receiving drug administration at 16 times required dose. Bereaved family claims 'no explanation of side-effects.' Tokyo Women's Medical University Hospital	Death of female in 40s	Female with brain tumor was administered anti-epileptic agent at 16 times the dose cited in the package insert, resulting in severe side-effects and death	Mainichi D
2014 Sept. 29	Death following detachment of gastric fistula tube Niigata City General Hospital	Death of male in 70s from peritonitis	Death due to detachment of gastric fistula tube. After transfer to another hospital, staff noticed and moved the patient to an emergency ward, but the patient died due to peritonitis and other complications. Mistakenly injected with air. Nutrients leaked out into the peritoneum and caused inflammation	Mainichi A
2014 Nov. 1	Male patient from Echizen City had gauze left in his body for over 15 years Fukui Prefectural Hospital	Male in 60s found to have foreign object in body	Surgical gauze was left behind in body of male patient that was discovered and removed some 15 years and 8 months later. After feeling mild pain under the lower right rib, the patient had an MRI scan at the same hospital which revealed a lump of gauze	Asahi A
2014 Nov. 5	Tube for liquid food supply entered airway Oe Kyōdō Hospital (currently Yoshinogawa Medical Center)	Death by asphyxiation of female in 90s	A female inpatient was found to have died of asphyxiation. A tube supplying liquid food to the stomach may have entered the airway, allowing liquid food to enter the lung and cause asphyxiation	Mainichi E

(continued)

Table 3.3 (continued)

Date	Accident or error / Name of medical institution	Injury or harm	Content of newspaper article (extract)	Source / Classification
2014 Nov. 22	Death of male left unattended for 70 min after sudden deterioration of cardiac failure. Staff failed to notice alarm sounding / Hyogo Prefectural Awaji Medical Center	Death of male in 70s	Male hospitalized for cardiac failure experienced a sudden deterioration, but although an alarm alerting to electrocardiographic abnormalities was sounding, the nurses failed to notice it for 72 min and the patient died. The hospital had turned down the volume setting	Mainichi / B
2014 Dec. 1	Death of male due to administration of muscle relaxant mistaken for antibacterial agent / Osaka General Medical Center	Death of male in 60s	The attending physician instructed drip infusion of the antibacterial agent maxipime, but the pharmacy mistakenly sent to the ward the muscle relaxant muscurate. The patient died 2 h later	Mainichi / D
2014 Dec. 13	Nurse made error in procedure for stopping infusion of painkiller / University of Yamanashi Hospital	Elderly female suffered cardiopulmonary arrest	While attempting to stop painkiller administration by drip infusion, the infusion pump circuit was disconnected but the circuit was not shut off, so that a large volume of painkiller entered the veins. The irregularity was noticed but the patient was already in a state of cardiopulmonary arrest	Mainichi / B
2014 Dec. 15	Former patient sued after being left unattended in the toilet and developing an infection / Taku City Hospital	93-year-old female developed hypothermia and urinary tract infection	Female in wheelchair was left unattended for a long period in the toilet and developed a urinary tract infection. The patient pressed the nurse call button but nobody noticed and she became hypothermic and developed a urinary tract infection	Mainichi / G

(continued)

Table 3.3 (continued)

Date	Accident or error Name of medical institution	Injury or harm	Content of newspaper article (extract)	Source Classification
2014 Dec. 19	Female resident of an elderly care facility died after being given the wrong medicine Special elderly nursing home in Saitama prefecture	Death of 88-year-old female	At breakfast, when giving a female an anti-hypertensive agent and other medicines, a staff member erroneously gave her a Parkinson's disease drug destined for another patient. Just over 1 h later, the patient vomited and died of aspiration pneumonia	Mainichi D
2015 Jan. 6	Gauze left in body Kobe City Medical Center General Hospital	Female in 40s. No sequelae	Gauze was left in female patient's brain for around 3 weeks. Infection led to cerebral abscess, which was removed by reoperation. The gauze had been left behind in surgery for partial resection of a tumor in the cerebral ventricle	Mainichi A
2015 Jan. 30	Misoperation of a drip infusion resulted in patient death. Large number of nurses without required knowledge. Kitakyushu Municipal Medical Center	Death of female in 90s from severe hemorrhage	After completion of drip infusion. mistaken operation resulted in severe hemorrhage. Many nurses were not aware of the risk of misoperation. The patient had been receiving treatment for urinary tract infection with continuous drip infusion	Asahi B
2015 Feb. 20	Metal cranial drill broke during surgery, fragment was left unnoticed for 2 months Hyogo Prefectural Kakogawa Medical Center	Female in 60s. No sequelae	During cranial surgery for subarachnoid hemorrhage in urgently hospitalized patient, the tip of a metal drill being used to bore a hole in the skull broke and a fragment was left in the skull. The accident was caused by a mistake in the type of drill used	Mainichi E

(continued)

Table 3.3 (continued)

Date	Accident or error / Name of medical institution	Injury or harm	Content of newspaper article (extract)	Source / Classification
2015 Feb. 24	6-year old girl accidentally inoculated with expired vaccine. Inadequate checking. Fujita General Hospital	6-year-old girl. No damage to health	Expired measles–rubella vaccine was mistakenly inoculated to one 6-year-old girl. The inoculation was given on February 24 but the expiry date of the vaccine was February 6. The accident was caused by inadequate checking	Mainichi / D
2015 Mar. 9	12 patients affected by swelling and pain at injection site / Private hospital in Miyoshi City, Hiroshima Prefecture	12 patients suffered symptoms such as swelling and pain at the injection site	A total of 12 patients who received block injection suffered symptoms including swelling and pain at the injection site. Of the 12, seven were found to have hemolytic streptococcus, which causes infection, strongly suggesting a medical accident	Asahi / D
2015 May 8	Death from fall during X-ray / Screening program of Numata City, Gunma Prefecture	Death of female in 50s	During stomach X-ray, female patient fell from table and died. It is claimed that staff neglected the duty to maintain vigilance using an observation window and monitor screen, resulting in death from hemorrhagic shock following cerebral artery damage	Mainichi / G
2015 May 12	Kidney damage due to mistaken catheter insertion / Mutsu General Hospital	Death of female in 70s	During changing of catheter of female patient, the inserted catheter penetrated as far as the kidney, resulting in death	Mainichi / A

(continued)

Table 3.3 (continued)

Date	Accident or error Name of medical institution	Injury or harm	Content of newspaper article (extract)	Source Classification
2015 May 22	Esophageal cancer was left untreated for 2 years and 5 months Niigata Prefectural Central Hospital	Esophageal cancer in male in 80s progressed and spread to lymph glands	After diagnosis of hypopharyngeal cancer and admission to the ear, nose and throat department, the patient underwent an endoscopic examination which showed that esophageal cancer was co-present. The discovery of esophageal cancer by the internist was however not passed on, and was also mis-entered in the electronic medical record	Mainichi F
2015 May 29	Excess administration of insulin, relationship to patient death unclear Shizuoka Cancer Center	Death of male in 60s	For a short period, insulin was administered at above the required dose, leading to a hypoglycemic state and consciousness disturbance resulting in death. The cause of death was reportedly maxillary cancer	Mainichi D
2015 May 29	Metal wire left in place after catheter insertion Kumamoto University Hospital	Female in hospital for premature birth. Sequelae unclear	After catheter insertion, stylet penetrated into the left thoracic cavity and was removed in surgical operation. The patient experienced severe pain in the torso. X-ray showed the stylet had penetrated the vein wall and passed into the left thoracic cavity	Asahi A
2015 June 2	Death of male at medical care facility after delayed arrival of ambulance due to control center mistake Sendai City Fire Department	Death of male in 60s	Control center mistake in which wrong address was given to emergency crew. Arrival at scene delayed by around 8 min. Patient died at medical care facility, but causative role of delay is unclear. On arrival the patient was already in a state of cardiopulmonary arrest	Mainichi H

(continued)

Table 3.3 (continued)

Date	Accident or error Name of medical institution	Injury or harm	Content of newspaper article (extract)	Source Classification
2015 June 17	Mistake in catheter insertion Mutsu General Hospital	Death of female in 80s	When catheter was inserted in vena cava in neck,it penetrated as far as the heart and caused blood reflux. Cardiopulmonary arrest resulting in death	Mainichi A
2015 June 30	Gauze left in stomach for 30 years. Case publicized. Niigata University Medical & Dental Hospital	Male in 80s found to have 5 cm of granular tissue on exterior wall of stomach	Gauze left in stomach for 30 years. Due to stomach ulcer, surgery to remove part of stomach was performed. Gauze was apparently left behind by mistake. When the male patient visited a separate hospital, a granular tissue growth was found on the stomach exterior	Asahi A
2015 July 1	Mistaken administration of formalin Steel Memorial Hirohata Hospital	Up to 56 people aged 10 to 80s incl. one man who suffered systemic neuralgia	Patients for endoscope examination were given formalin fluid mistaken for purified water. The mistake affected up to 56 patients aged from 10 to 80s. One male patient complained of health damage and still suffers sequelae including systemic neuralgia	Mainichi A
2015 July 24	Lenses were placed in the wrong eye in cataract surgery Niigata University Medical & Dental Hospital	Female in 80s with cataracts	Female in 80s had surgery to insert in both eyes a lens to adjust visual strength. As a result of an investigation in response to complaints from the patient, it was found that the lenses were each in the wrong eye	Mainichi A

(continued)

Table 3.3 (continued)

Date	Accident or error Name of medical institution	Injury or harm	Content of newspaper article (extract)	Source Classification
2015 July 30	Catheters re-used in 300 patients over 5-year period after sterilization Kobe University Hospital	Around 296 patients were affected over a period of around 5 years from 2010	Medical catheters were re-used against government ordinance. Re-use occurred in around 296 patients over the period of around 5 years from 2010 for which records are available. Re-use is not ruled out in a further 41	Mainichi B
2015 Aug. 1	Mistake in drip infusion resulted in patient death from blood loss. Inadequate checking of device handling. Kitakyushu Municipal Medical Center	Death from blood loss of patient in 90s	Wrong procedure for detaching drip infusion tube resulted in death of female patient from blood loss. When nurse detached drug supply tube from device, the connector tube attached to its tip was also detached	Mainichi B
2015 Aug. 17	Infant death due to misjudgment of ambulance crew during urgent transportation for cardiopulmonary arrest Fire Department, Sasebo City, Nagasaki Prefecture	Death of 10-month old infant	During urgent transport of a 10-month old male infant in cardiopulmonary arrest, misreading of electrocardiogram led to mistake in emergency procedure through failure to use a defibrillator, which attempts to restart heartbeat using electric pulses. Infant died after arrival at hospital	Mainichi F
2015 Aug. 18	Healthy ovary removed along with unhealthy one Ohsaki Citizen Hospital	Female in 30s had ovary removed by mistake	In surgery to remove right ovary of female in 30s, the healthy left ovary was also removed. Before the start of surgery, it was confirmed that the tumor-affected right ovary was to be resected, but the surgery was carried out using a laparoscope attached to a monitor screen	Asahi F

(continued)

Table 3.3 (continued)

Date	Accident or error Name of medical institution	Injury or harm	Content of newspaper article (extract)	Source Classification
2015 Sept. 29	Mistake in insulin administration Shizuoka Cancer Center	Male in 60s suffered consciousness disturbance and death	Terminal cancer patient with history of diabetes mellitus was given an excessive dose of insulin within a short period. Patient died. In order to stabilize symptoms with treatment, injections were given 5 times at intervals of around 30 min	Mainichi D
2015 Sept.	Oversight in cancer test, left untreated for 11 months Niigata Cancer Center Hospital	Male in 70s. Patient survived	The results of an imaging test showing a finding of cancer were overlooked by the treating doctor, and appropriate treatment was not given for 11 months	Mainichi F
2015 Oct.	Oversight in cancer test, treatment delayed by half a year Niigata Cancer Center Hospital	Female in 60s. Patient survived	The results of an imaging test showing a finding of cancer were overlooked by the treating doctor, treatment was delayed for half a year	Mainichi F
2015 Nov. 8	Surgical mistake left male in 50s with nerve damage Gunma University Hospital	Persistent nerve damage in male in 50s	In orthopedic surgery to fix bones in neck of male patient in 50s, surgical screw was mistakenly inserted into spinal canal through which the nerve travels	Mainichi A
2015 Nov. 20	Patient death after falling from examining table and being crushed Daiyukai General Hospital	Death of female in 70s	Female patient (74) fell from examining table, torso became caught between moving parts of investigative equipment and she died of asphyxiation. The patient had been secured to the examining table, but began to move immediately after start of the procedure and died from crushing of the chest and abdomen	Mainichi E

(continued)

Table 3.3 (continued)

Date	Accident or error Name of medical institution	Injury or harm	Content of newspaper article (extract)	Source Classification
2015 Nov.	Patient death after fall from bed, complaint by bereaved family Kochi Health Sciences Center	Death of 29-year-old male	Fall from bed caused brain damage and unconsciousness and death 3 months later. Male hospitalized for severe respiratory failure, fell out of bed next day. The patient suffered severe knock to the head, fell unconscious, and died	Asahi C
2015 Dec. 25	Mastectomy after confusion of samples Chiba Cancer Center	Right breast of female in 30s erroneously removed	Just as the hospital was rebuilding trust after issues with a series of patient deaths in laparoscopic surgery, a complete mastectomy was wrongly carried out due to the elementary mistake of confusion of samples	Mainichi F
2015 Dec. 25	Gauze left for 27 years in bone in leg of female in 60s Niigata Prefectural Shibata Hospital	Female in 60s. No sequelae	Gauze left for 27 years in bone in leg. Patient had surgery at a different hospital after complaining of pain in leg, whereupon the gauze was discovered and surgically removed	Asahi E
2015 Dec.	Severe hemorrhage due to surgical mistake Chiba Cancer Center	Male in 60s had successful surgery but hemorrhaged three times	In surgery to remove esophagus, mishandling of instrument by doctor led to difficulties with hemostasis and severe hemorrhage of around 2 l, which the patient was not informed of. Reported to prefecture as medical accident	Mainichi E

(continued)

Table 3.3 (continued)

Date	Accident or error Name of medical institution	Injury or harm	Content of newspaper article (extract)	Source Classification
2015 Dec.	Gauze left behind unnoticed for 2 months due to miscounting by nurse during surgery Chiba Cancer Center	Female in 60s, readmitted to hospital after intestinal blockage	Medical error in which medical gauze was left in body after surgery to remove kidney cancer, discovered in test 2 months later. During surgery, nurse miscounted number of sheets, doctor also failed to notice in X-ray the next day	Mainichi E
2015	Mistake in drug administration possibly connected to death of child University of Tokyo Hospital	Death of pre-school male child	Accident occurred during injection of internal medication into the stomach of a male child in serious condition from multiple organ damage. After preparing injection, nurse interrupted procedure to answer telephone, etc. On resuming, mistakenly took up internal medication intended for other nearby patient	Mainichi B
2016 Jan. 17	Female death after colon injury due to surgical mistake Funabashi Orthopedic Hospital	Death of female in 50s	Death of female in 50s three days after mistake had caused colon injury. Surgery was a new technique known as XLIF in which a hole of around 2 cm diameter is opened in the side of the abdomen to insert medical instruments	Mainichi A
2016 May 24	Disinfectant accidentally placed on humidifier Meitetsu Hospital	One-year old male child. No damage to health	Child was in hospital with pneumonia. The bed was completely covered with an oxygen tent, but the nurse put into the tent's humidifier 40 ml of disinfectant mistaken for purified water	Mainichi B

(continued)

Table 3.3 (continued)

Date	Accident or error Name of medical institution	Injury or harm	Content of newspaper article (extract)	Source Classification
2016 May 30	Wrong transplant site used in intervertebral surgery Ōgaki Municipal Hospital	Male in 50s had walking difficulty from limb numbness due to intervertebral hernia	Wrong site was operated on in intervertebral surgery. Patient underwent surgery to remove the damaged disk and transplant bone into the lower back. The doctor in charge made a visual error, the surgeon also failed to check and transplanted to a different site	Mainichi F
2016 July 8	Mistake in surgery on cervical vertebrae resulting in damage to patient arm and leg Gunma University Hospital	Male in 50s left with damage to right arm and leg	Male patient had paralysis of hand and leg and received surgery to fix vertebrae in the back of the head and neck. The surgeon mistook the fixing site of the screws and compressed the spinal cord. Damage reportedly persisted despite immediate reoperation	Mainichi A
2016 July 21	Mishandling of instruments during surgery Chiba Cancer Center	Male in 60s. No sequelae	Mistaken operation of hemostasis equipment during surgery on esophageal cancer patient due to inexperienced nurse. Hemostasis did not function properly using the equipment and the doctor used a different method	Mainichi E
2016 July 21	Female infant of 3 months suffered brain damage in heart surgery Keio University Hospital	3-month-old female infant became bedbound	During surgery, insertion site of tube conveying blood from heart-lung machine was inappropriate leading to interruption of blood supply to brain. Staff failed to notice due to neglect of duty of vigilance	Mainichi A

(continued)

Table 3.3 (continued)

Date	Accident or error Name of medical institution	Injury or harm	Content of newspaper article (extract)	Source Classification
2016 Aug. 10	Theft of hard disk containing 15,000 patient information files Isesaki Municipal Hospital	Theft of 15,000 patient information files	Female employee returning to company housing in Ageo City, Saitama Prefecture, took with her hard disk and papers containing information and left them in her car. On noticing the theft she reported it	Mainichi F
2016 Aug. 12	3-month-old infant develops fever after mistaken inoculation of vaccine Clinic in Hokkaido	3-month-old female infant developed fever. No sequelae	3-month-old infant was mistakenly inoculated with Japanese encephalitis vaccine designed for children of 6 months or above. The child receiving the wrong inoculation developed a fever of 38.7, which apparently resolved in the morning	Mainichi D
2016 Aug. 12	Patient with intractable disease was left unattended in toilet, died one month later Imazu Red Cross Hospital	Death of female in 60s	Female left alone in toilet when nursing assistant went to attend to another task is thought to have lost consciousness and was found around 2 h later in a state of cardiopulmonary arrest and died several days later. The message that the patient needed to be constantly attended had not been passed on	Mainichi F
2016 Aug. 18	Gauze left in abdomen of patient in 60s during stomach surgery Minami Wakayama Medical Center	Male in 60s. No damage to health	Sheet of gauze left in abdomen of male patient who underwent stomach surgery. This was caused by neglect of the rule requiring confirmation of the number of sheets of gauze during surgery. Gauze removed 5 days later	Asahi A

(continued)

Table 3.3 (continued)

Date	Accident or error Name of medical institution	Injury or harm	Content of newspaper article (extract)	Source Classification
2016 Sept. 1	Death 2 days after surgery. Reported to investigative body. Hikone Municipal Hospital	Patient death	Patient underwent surgery and died 2 days later. During surgery on the first of the month, patient suffered sudden loss of blood pressure and died on the 3rd. Before surgery, the hospital had not informed the patient and family of the risk of death	Mainichi E
2016 Sept. 13	Death of male following failure to communicate signs of cancer Nagoya University Hospital	Death of male in 50s from lung cancer	Despite signs of lung cancer, failure by doctors to share information led to male patient's death 2 years later. Report on imaging diagnosis was prepared but doctor did not refer to it or report its content to the patient	Mainichi F
2016 Sept. 16	Diagnosis and surgery based on confusion of samples of two female patients. Yamagata Prefectural Central Hospital	Female in 40s and female in 80s. Neither patient showed metastasis	Samples were confused between female patient in 40s with phyllodes tumor in breast and female breast cancer patient in 80s. Surgery was thus based on the wrong test results in each case. No cancer metastasis was observed	Mainichi F
2016 Sept. 23	Death of female in 80s due to tenfold insulin overdose Nagasaki Kawatana Medical Center	Death of female in 80s	Insulin was administered to inpatient at 10 times dose ordered by doctor. Patient subsequently died	Mainichi D

(continued)

Table 3.3 (continued)

Date	Accident or error Name of medical institution	Injury or harm	Content of newspaper article (extract)	Source Classification
2016 Nov. 8	Damage to superior vena cava during lung surgery Nagoya City University Hospital	Female in 50s died of hemorrhagic shock and multi-organ failure	Female patient died during lung cancer surgery. During operation to remove the inferior lobe of the right lung of a female in 50s from Nagoya, the superior vena cava was accidentally damaged, causing severe hemorrhage the next day. The patient died of hemorrhagic shock and multi-organ failure	Mainichi A
2016 Dec.	Gauze left for 11 years in body Takarazuka City Hospital	Female in 50s. Made complete recovery	Sheet of hemostatic gauze found in body of female in 50s who had had breast cancer surgery 11 years earlier. Patient noticed suppuration close to the surgical suture site, and the gauze was found on hospital inspection	Mainichi A

Chapter 4
Supplymentary: Categories in Survey Report on Japanese Medical Accidents

4.1 Big Data Protocol of Medical Accidents and Errors

The gathering of information on medical accidents in Japan began in response to the 2004 amendment of the Medical Services Law, which made the reporting of medical accidents compulsory, and is led chiefly by the Japan Council for Quality Health Care. The scope of compulsory reporting is defined by the Council as indicated below:

① Cases of clearly identified erroneous medical treatment or management where such treatment or management results in patient death or lasting physical or psychological harm to the patient or makes necessary treatment measures or other therapies that are either unforeseen or exceed the foreseen range.

② Cases where erroneous medical treatment or management is not clearly identified but where the medical treatment or management carried out results in patient death or lasting physical or psychological harm to the patient or makes necessary treatment measures or other therapies that are either unforeseen or exceed the foreseen range (including cases suspected to be the result of the medical treatment or management carried out, but only where the consequences are unforeseen).

③ In addition to cases covered by ① and ② above, examples which may contribute to the prevention of accidents within medical institutions or to the prevention of accident recurrence.

Cases are analyzed by the Council and are published in four quarterly reports and an annual report. In each reporting year, an analysis theme is set, and education is carried out focusing on cases with high rates of recurrence as part of measures to publicize the issue of medical safety among medical personnel. There are detailed reports on cases other than those from the newspaper articles featured in the medical

© The Author(s), under exclusive license to Springer Nature Singapore Pte Ltd. 2019   71
S. Atsuji, *Resilience Management for a Sustainable Aging Society*,
SpringerBriefs in Business, https://doi.org/10.1007/978-981-13-5805-0_4

accident big data presented above, with the central focus on issues related to medical intervention (A. Medical intervention, B. Nursing intervention). The other medical accidents factors presented in the data list above (C. Patient action, D. Management of medical drugs and instruments, E. Team treatment, F. Medical information management, G. Hospital management, H. Community medicine, I. Medical policy) and related issues are however beyond the scope of the reports. Below are presented the outline contents of the medical accident reports published by the Division of Adverse Event Prevention of the Japan Council for Quality Health Care.

4.2   Abstract Data: Medical Accident and Errors 2000–2011 (Above Shown 2012–2016)

Newspaper article data on 439 Japanese medical accidents in the period 2000–2016 were subjected to text mining and the degree of correlation among terms appearing with high frequency in the articles was analyzed. The following general clusters were identified (a) unconscious/condition; (b) mistake/tube/breathing; (c) bleeding/high volume; (d) failure/organ; (e) administration (drug); (f) test; (g) gauze/excision/internal. From these clusters was identified the frequency of 'high-risk accident patterns'. Meanwhile, each cluster corresponded to elements requiring particular and constant attention in the clinical setting, and can be seen as a checkpoint associated with high risk of medical accidents. The treatment in the newspaper articles concentrated on drastic medical accidents of high newsworthiness that grab public attention but errors, mistakes, incidents, and misunderstandings seem to move out of focus with the passing of time.

① **Editorial policy (data published in newspapers)**:

Included in the survey were all recorded data on medical accidents and errors published in newspapers from 2012 to 2016 (105 cases). The names of doctors, nurses and other medical personnel and patients are omitted for the sake of protecting privacy as the present research will in the future be subject to big-data macro-analysis aimed at reducing medical accidents. However, to make it possible to identify the specific newspaper article, establish that the incident is based on fact rather than invention, and verify the facts of the matter and its background, the names of the medical institutions and hospitals where the medical accidents and errors occurred are reproduced as they appeared in the newspaper (the results of medical litigation and disputes in individual incidents are not included). In the case of each medical accident or error, including in cases where concealment and falsification led to a delay in detection, public attention, and newspaper coverage, the date adopted is that on which the accident is reported by the newspaper to have occurred.

② **Classification range of medical accidents and errors (major categories)**:

The data included are articles published in newspapers that are chiefly concerned with medical accidents or medical errors, and excluding incidents, errors, and misunderstandings. In accordance with the classification of the Japanese MHLW, only cases where the facts of the accident are clearly documented in newspaper articles were covered. The principles of classification of the various categories of medical accident, medical error, etc., vary widely from country to country including among the medically advanced nations of North America and Europe.

③ **Analytical methodology for medical accidents and errors**:

The source data published in newspapers regarding medical accidents and errors were subjected to the following analyses: (i) the number of accidents for each of the years 2012–2016 was visualized by accident cause in a three-dimensional figure; (ii) the data were classified by stratification according to accident cause (shown in Mandala of Failure); (iii) all newspaper articles on medical accidents were mapped by text mining and their characteristics analysed by creating a medical accident big database. The analytical content of the present Medical Accidents and Errors 2012–2016 is discussed in the separate document ICT Resilience Management for Sustainable Aging Society: Medical Accidents Preventability using Big-data.

④ **Sourcing of articles and data on medical accidents and errors**:

Documentary material relating to medical accidents and errors was drawn exclusively from articles published in the Mainichi Shimbun, Yomiuri Shimbun, Asahi Shimbun, and Nihon Keizai Shimbun newspapers. Regarding the terminology used in the different newspapers, in addition to the specific terms concealment (*inpei*) and falsification (*kaizan*), the two terms for nurse *kangofu* and *kangoshi* are also both used in line with the article content as they appear therein.

⑤ **Data structuring of medical accident list and creation of big database**:

The order of data is as follows: date, name of medical institution where accident or error occurred, description of resulting injury or harm, content of newspaper article (extract), source/classification. The creation of a big database of medical accidents and errors was performed through text mining of 'accumulated unstructured data' published in newspapers from 2012 to 2016, which allowed a visualization of the developing trend of medical accidents over 17 years from 2000 to 2016.

4.3 Medical Accident Classification Criteria

The critieria for classification of the cause of medical accidents and errors were as set out below (the classification symbol appears in the table below the indication of the source.)

A: *Medical intervention*

Refers to diagnosis and surgical treatment, drug prescription, or other action for the purpose of treatment of disease or injury. This includes for example cases where surgical gauze is inadvertently left in the body after an operation, or where injection is given at the wrong site.

B: *Nursing intervention*

Refers to the general range of nursing action to support the patient as an auxiliary to the above-mentioned medical intervention, but excluding medical intervention itself. For example, cases where the wrong intravenous drip drug is administered or where an artificial respirator is inadvertently not connected to the power source.

C: *Patient action*

Refers to accidents arising from the patient's own action. Includes, for example, falls in the hospital, falling out of bed, refusing medical intervention, violence against medical professionals, or other action to obstruct medical intervention. It additionally includes cases where the patient seeks a second opinion from one or more other medical institutions and receives a range of different treatments and prescriptions, resulting in multi-drug co-medication unintended by the patient or the medical personnel.

D: *Medical drug- or medical instrument-related*

Refers to the administration, infusion, or preparation of medical drugs, including anesthetic preparations for surgery, or action for the management of medication or medical treatment. This includes for example misunderstandings over preparation of drug mixtures or drug concentration and cases where drugs are administered after their expiry date, or where the wrong drug is administered. It also includes mishandling of medical instruments supplied by medical manufacturers and defects or flaws in the instruments themselves.

E: *Team treatment*

Refers to secondary medical intervention such as testing, diagnosis, and surgical support, including by technical staff (e.g. clinical engineers) auxiliary to surgery, but excluding nursing intervention. This includes for example cases where surgery is carried out based on confusion of test results with those of a different patient and cases where someone other than the staff member responsible undertakes medical intervention with undesired results. Particularly in the advanced medical treatment of today, where it is essential for medical treatment institutions to handle the latest medical instruments and ensure coordination between team members, overall team capability is required.

F: *Medical information management*

Refers to the general range of information management relating to medical systems, including for instance management of general patient information, staff shift patterns, overwork, and allocation of tasks. This includes for example mis-inputting of electronic records and prescription notes, miscommunication of information between medical professionals, and misunderstandings over accident information. It also includes injury due to multi-drug co-medication or application of different treatment measures in elderly patients consulting multiple medical institutions (there are also cases where patients seeking a second opinion are prescribed different drugs at a number of different hospitals).

G: *Hospital management*

Refers to governance aspects of national, public, and private university hospitals, medical institutions, and medical corporations. This includes for example cases of continued long-term use of obsolete technology or long-term re-use of non-re-usable medical instruments. It further includes inability of personnel systems to cope adequately with night-time or emergency admissions due to cost-cutting, regardless of whether at an emergency or a regular medical institution.

H: *Community medicine*

Refers to coordination with the local community by medical institutions and medical corporations, whether public or private. This includes, for example, cases where communication issues in emergency response lead to delay in arrival of ambulances, or buck-passing of responsibility for emergency patients at the boundaries between the jurisdictions of different prefectural-level authorities.

I: *Medical policy*

Refers to the medical policy and health administration exercised by central government (MHLW) and the healthcare facilities of local government authorities. This includes the general range of policy issues and systemic issues, exemplified by the spread of hepatitis B and hepatitis C infection through a preventive immunization campaign and other central government measures.

4.4 Medical Accidents and Errors 2000–2011 (Abstract)

See, whole data following Table 4.1.

Table 4.1 Medical accidents and errors 2000–2011 (abstract)

Date	Accident or error Name of medical institution	Injury or harm	Content of newspaper article (extract)	Source Classification
2000 Jan. 20	Injury to esophagus during gastroscopy Kasugai Municipal Hospital	39-year-old male hospitalized for approx. 6 weeks	After gastroscopy examination by a doctor in digestive medicine dept., the patient complained of chest pains. A test showed injury to the esophagus and inflammation	Asahi A
2000 Jan. 22	Respiratory arrest leading to death. Hospital director cited 'misoperation' National Sanatorium Matsue Hospital (Currently Matsue Medical Center)	Death of female elementary school sixth-grader	An assistant nurse switched the artificial respirator off to attend to the patient, but was not sure whether it was switched back on afterwards. The hospital considered it likely that she forgot to restart the machine	Asahi B
2000 Jan. 27	Patient death due to surgical mistake. Injury to small intestine during gall bladder removal Ohana Daiichi Hospital, Naha	Death of male patient due to co-occurrence of septicemia and multi-organ failure	An endoscope was inserted into the abdomen and the gall bladder resected. After surgery, the patient complained of abdominal pain. On reoperation a 1 cm long injury to the small intestine was found. The patient developed peritonitis and died the next day	Asahi A
2000 Jan.	Damage to artery during surgery, right leg amputated afterward Niigata Cancer Center Hospital	Amputation of right leg of female patient	During surgery on to insert an artificial knee joint, the doctor, while attempting to drill a hole in the right femur to immobilize the joint, inflicted an injury on the artery. Subsequently, the right leg was amputated below the knee	Asahi A
2000 Jan.	Patient death due to injection of nutrient into blood vessel Mahoshi Hospital	Death of 76-year-old female from acute respiratory failure	The patient had a nutrient tube in the abdomen and a drip infusion tube in the right arm, but the nurse mistakenly injected the nutrient through the drip infusion tube into the blood vessel	Asahi B
2000 Feb. 1	Corneal transplant from patient infected with hepatitis C due to hospital's double mistake Gunma University Hospital	Cornea of hepatitis C patient transplanted to two other patients	Cornea provided by patient infected with hepatitis C virus was transplanted to two other patients. Not only did hospital not immediately dispose of problem cornea, but also doctor did not check whether it was suitable for surgery	Asahi G
2000 Feb. 5	Death of male possibly caused by anesthetic mistake Municipal hospital in Himeji City	Death of 46-year-old male	Toward the end of surgery for empyema, male became unconscious. It was found among other issues that there was no oxygen in the left lung. Suspected issues in securing of airway and intubation method	Asahi A
2000 Feb. 11	Surgery for digital correction on right leg applied to the wrong (left) leg Hachinohe City Hospital	Surgery on female patient applied to wrong site	In joint fixing surgery to correct a digit on the patient's right leg, surgery was mistakenly performed on the left leg. On the day of surgery, the operating surgeon was changed at short notice. The substituting doctor misread 'right' as 'left' on the surgery notes	Asahi F

(continued)

Table 4.1 (continued)

Date	Accident or error Name of medical institution	Injury or harm	Content of newspaper article (extract)	Source Classification
2000 Feb.	Patient death due to antiseptic fluid mistaken for distilled water and used in respirator Kyoto University Hospital	Death of 17-year-old female due to ethanol poisoning	Humidifier unit of artificial respirator was mistakenly filled with antiseptic ethanol instead of distilled water and other infectious disease symptoms became aggravated. The hospital failed to apply urgent treatment for alcohol poisoning and the patient died	Asahi E
2000 Apr. 4	Male became temporarily unconscious after injection into vein of intestinal agent Hashimoto City National Health Insurance Hospital (Currently Hashimoto City Hospital)	Male in 70s fell into serious state of temporary unconsciousness	Intestinal agent should have been injected through nutrient tube via nose, but the nurse mistakenly introduced it through the drip infusion tube. The nurse noticed the mistake immediately and stopped the procedure, but the patient fell temporarily unconscious	Asahi B
2000 Apr. 9	Patient death due to drip infusion of medicine for oral use. Apology to bereaved family for 'mistake' Tokai University Hospital	Death of 18-month-old female child	A preparation for internal use consisting of seven agents including a therapeutic bronchodilator and antibiotics was mistakenly given by the nurse through drip infusion. Immediately after infusion began, the child's face turned blue, her nose bled, and she died	Asahi B
2000 Apr. 17	Patient fell into serious condition following accident during endoscopic examination Ōdate Municipal General Hospital	83-year-old female developed serious condition	During examination with an endoscope known as an epipharyngoscope, the tapered tip of the endoscope punctured the internal wall of the esophagus, injuring the mediastinum. The injured mediastinum suppurated, became inflamed and the condition gradually worsened	Asahi A
2000 May 25	Sudden death due to detachment of respiratory support device Ishikiri Seiki Hospital	Death of 61-year-old male	It was discovered that the tube and drip infusion needle of a respiratory support device attached to patient had become detached. They were immediately reattached, but the patient died	Asahi E
2000 Jun. 2	Surgery performed on misidentified patient due to miscopying of patient number University of Tsukuba Hospital	Surgery carried out with confused identities of males in 30s and 60s	The wrong patient number was written on a vial containing tissue sampled before surgery, so that surgery was carried out on the basis of the test results of a different lung cancer patient tested on the same day	Asahi F
2000 Jun. 8	Sudden death of patient possibly due to overdose of drip infusion Tokai University Hospital	Death of 52-year-old male	Sudden death of male patient hospitalized for heart disease. Strong likelihood that the hospital mistakenly gave an overdose of drip infusion medication, causing heart failure and arrhythmia	Asahi A
2000 Jun.	Hole in colon during surgery Hakodate Central General Hospital	Death of 69-year-old male	During intestinal polypectomy, a hole appeared in the colon, but the treating doctor failed to notice and subsequently took inappropriate measures. Laparotomy was performed on a later day but the patient developed severe peritonitis and died	Asahi A

(continued)

Table 4.1 (continued)

Date	Accident or error Name of medical institution	Injury or harm	Content of newspaper article (extract)	Source Classification
2000 Jun.	Patient death after vomiting of blood during endoscopic examination Moji Hospital	Death of 85-year-old male	As the patient continued to bring up blood, an endoscope was inserted and a gelatinous substance found in the lung, which the doctor attempted to remove with a forceps at the tip of the endoscope. After the endoscope was withdrawn, the patient vomited large amounts of blood and died	Asahi A
2000 Jul. 4	Mistake during cancer resection, reoperation for removal Aichi Cancer Center	Female in 50s. No health damage ensued	Surgery was performed after examination confirmed cancer cells in colon. However, pathological examination of the resected tissue discovered no cancer tissue, and that a polyp at another site had been mistaken for the cancer and removed	Asahi A
2000 Jul. 5	Artificial respirator became detached, patient died 17 days later Iwata City Hospital	Death of 49-year-old male	Tube of artificial respirator attached to patient became detached due to nurse mistake and other causes, putting patient life at risk. The patient survived the initial crisis, but his blood pressure gradually dropped and he died subsequently	Asahi B
2000 Jul. 6	Male patient developed peritonitis after surgery for bowel obstruction and died Takamatsu Hospital of the National Sanatorium (Currently Takamatsu Medical Center)	Death of 53-year-old male	The patient was diagnosed with bowel obstruction and received surgery to remove the obstructed section. However, after surgery, due to onset of peritonitis and other reasons, he was reoperated, but died at the hospital to which he was transferred	Asahi A
2000 Jul. 31	Drug and patient name were not recorded, leading to injection to wrong patient Nihon University Itabashi Hospital	Death of 89-year-old male	A nurse failed to follow the procedural manual and did not write the name of the drug and patient on the syringe. The intern doctor also failed to check the syringe content and injected the patient with another patient's medicine, leading to death	Asahi E
2000 Jul.	Drip infusion of sleep medication leaves patient in vegetative state Higashiosaka City Medical Center	Vegetative state in 61-year-old male	A patient with chronic respiratory failure due to pneumonia was given drip infusion of sleep medication by a nurse who failed to notice the doctor's instruction. The patient fell into a vegetative state	Asahi F
2000 Aug. 2	Patient fell into vegetative state after oxygen tube became detached Fujiyoshida Municipal Medical Center	Male in 50s fell into vegetative state	An oxygen tube was inserted after surgery on the trachea. When the patient's position was changed for examination, the tube became detached. Reinitubation was carried out, but a vegetative state ensued due to insufficient oxygen supply to brain	Asahi E
2000 Aug. 14	Patient developed pneumonia after liquid nutrient infiltrated artificial respirator National Hospital Organization Miyazaki Higashi Hospital	Two-year-old male child developed pneumonia	A nurse who tried to pour liquid nutrient, etc., into the mouth of a tube into the child's stomach mistakenly poured it into the cleaning port of the artificial respirator instead. The error was noticed and measures taken, but the patient developed pneumonia	Asahi B

(continued)

Table 4.1 (continued)

Date	Accident or error / Name of medical institution	Injury or harm	Content of newspaper article (extract)	Source Classification
2000 Aug. 14	Nurse neglected procedure and made a mistake in transfusion / Ōdate Municipal General Hospital	No health damage ensued	A transfusion of a red blood cell preparation intended for another male patient with the same blood disease in the next bed who had blood group O was given by a nurse to a male patient with blood group A. The patient noticed the mistake and immediately stopped the transfusion himself	Asahi B
2000 Aug. 21	Double administration of anticancer agents / University of Tsukuba Hospital	Drastic fall in infant's white blood cell and platelet counts, reduced immune resistance	An intern doctor injected the anticancer agent vincristine sulfate. However, as the doctor did not record the administration in the instruction memo, approx. 1 h later another intern doctor gave the same injection again	Asahi A
2000 Aug. 26	Nutrient administered into vein due to drip infusion mistake / Kobayashi Hospital	Death of 87-year-old female	An assistant nurse gave a nutrient via a tube attached to the connector of a drip infusion in the right arm, so that the nutrient, which should have been fed straight into the stomach, entered the drip infusion, causing acute circulatory failure and death	Asahi B
2000 Sept. 27	Doctor misread dose, leading to death / Saitama Medical Center	Death of 16-year-old female high-school pupil	A drug supposed to be given at 2 ml a week was mistakenly given at 2 ml a day, leading to side-effects of high fever, muscle pains, and platelet reduction. The medical team discontinued the medication, but the patient did not recover	Asahi E
2000 Sept.	Patient death following mistaken insertion of nutrition tube into lung / Morioka Red Cross Hospital	Death of female in 90s	A nurse mistakenly inserted into the trachea a plastic nutrition tube intended for the stomach, leading to patient death	Asahi B
2000 Oct. 21	Patient death during surgery due to erroneous attachment of breathing apparatus / Kobe University Hospital	Death of 64-year-old female	When a so-called peep valve was attached to the anesthetic apparatus due to breathing difficulties, the anesthesiologist fitted the valve for the outlet direction to the inlet direction, so that sufficient oxygen was unable to reach the lung	Asahi A
2000 Oct. 24	Screw left in body after surgery / JA Fuchu General Hospital (Currently Fuchu City Hospital)	Screw from medical instrument left in body of 25-year-old female for approx. 6 weeks	After appendicitis surgery, one metallic screw was found. The screw was part of a medical instrument to drain cleaning fluid and other substances collecting in the abdomen. During surgery, it became detached from the instrument and fell into the body. Has now been removed	Asahi E
2000 Oct.	Injury to spine during surgery on lower back caused ankle paralysis / Fukui Prefectural Hospital	71-year-old male left with paralysis	A patient undergoing lower back surgery was left with ankle paralysis. The hospital held a press conference and acknowledged the mistake. The cause was explained as injury due to contact of a surgical drill with the spinal nerve	Asahi A

(continued)

Table 4.1 (continued)

Date	Accident or error Name of medical institution	Injury or harm	Content of newspaper article (extract)	Source Classification
2000 Oct.	Inflammation caused by gastroscopy Shimokita Medical Center Ohata Hospital	Death of 69-year-old male	During endoscopic examination, the gastroscope would not pass through the throat, and the procedure was abandoned after three attempts. However, the gastroscope apparently caused injury to the esophagus, resulting in inflammation. The patient was transferred to another hospital for continued treatment but died	Asahi A
2000 Dec. 14	Death following administration of hemostatic agent Public Soma General Hospital	Death of 74-year-old male	In line with doctor's instructions, nurse prepared hemostatic agent for nasal administration, but asked another nurse to administer it, who failed to confirm the contents and administration method and carried out drip infusion, causing patient death	Asahi B
2001 Jan. 5	Transfusion mistake by intern doctor led to patient death next day University of Fukui Hospital	Death of 60-year-old female	As patient's circulation was poor, a plasma transfusion was decided. However, the patient, who had blood type B, was given O-type plasma. The transfusion mistake was claimed not to be the cause of death	Asahi E
2001 Jan. 19	Patient death from heavy bleeding after surgery Fukushima Prefectural Ono Hospital	Death of 76-year-old female	After suturing following surgery to insert an artificial bone in the hip joint, the doctor noticed a fall in blood pressure and on investigation discovered internal bleeding. Transfusion and other life-saving measures were taken but the patient did not recover	Asahi A
2001 Feb. 2	Mistake in drug administration led to death 2 days later Shinshu University Hospital	Death of male in 50s	Nurse confused a syringe containing sedative for a patient in treatment for serious collagen disease with one containing cardiotonic drug for a different patient, and attached the latter to the syringe pump. The patient's blood pressure fell and he died	Asahi B
2001 Feb. 15	Patient death after colon examination due to endoscope causing hole in intestinal wall Odate Municipal General Hospital	Death of 62-year-old female	A hole was mistakenly opened in the patient's colon wall during endoscopic examination. The patient fell into a state of reduced consciousness and later shock and died of peritonitis and other complications	Asahi A
2001 Feb.	Due to mistake in anesthetic administration, patient fell temporarily unconscious and developed pneumonia. Fukushima Medical University Hospital	Female in 80s temporarily unconscious but recovered	When the duty orthopedic surgeon inserted a tube for analgesic, it penetrated as far as the lumen of the dura mater, so that the drug was over-effective and the patient fell unconscious and developed aspiration pneumonia	Asahi A

(continued)

Table 4.1 (continued)

Date	Accident or error Name of medical institution	Injury or harm	Content of newspaper article (extract)	Source Classification
2001 Mar. 2	Patient death due to misinsertion of liquid nutrient tube Sado National Sanatorium (Currently Mano-Mizuho Hospital)	Death of 76-year-old female	The patient was unable to eat while treated for gastric fistula. When the doctor replaced the tube with a new one, the patient complained of pain. Examination showed that the tube had been inserted between the outer wall of the stomach and the peritoneum	Asahi A
2001 Mar. 2	Misoperation of artificial heart lung machine during heart surgery Tokyo Women's Medical University Hospital	Death of 12-year-old patient	Due to insufficient blood drainage during surgery for atrial septal defect and pulmonary artery stenosis, severe brain damage occurred and death three days after surgery. At the time, no clinical engineer was present, and the accident was caused by the doctor's misoperation of the artificial heart lung machine	Asahi E
2001 Apr.	Miscarriage due to drip infusion mistake Gonohe General Hospital	Pregnant female suffered miscarriage	Drip infusion medication was wrongly prepared and administered without the mistake being noticed, leading to miscarriage. The result of a series of mistakes, including that a different medication to the one specified on the form was prepared and that the mistake went unnoticed at the time of the drip infusion	Asahi E
2001 Jun. 5	Patient death from transfusion mistake due to neglect of double check Niigata Prefectural Central Hospital	Death of male from multi-organ failure	Patient with blood type O bled heavily from the stomach wall during endoscopic examination. The doctor performed urgent surgery for hemostasis, but mistakenly gave a transfusion of type A blood, causing death from multi-organ failure	Asahi A
2001 Jun. 10	Removal of catheter forgotten, removed in reoperation Nagoya City University Hospital	80-year-old female. No sequelae	The doctor used a hemodialysis catheter with a twin-tube structure to carry out a large transfusion during surgery. When another doctor replaced it with a narrow catheter after surgery, he forgot to remove the internal tube	Asahi A
2001 Jun. 11	Patient death after tube became detached Yao Municipal Hospital	Death of 68-year-old male	After surgery to widen the coronary artery, arterial pressure was monitored with a measuring instrument connected by tube to the artery, but the tube became detached, causing heavy bleeding. The patient fell unconscious and died	Asahi E
2001 Aug. 9	Vegetative state ensued after tongue surgery due to delay in ensuring breathing Nagasaki University Dental School Hospital (Currently Nagasaki University Hospital)	23-year-old female fell into vegetative state	The patient was diagnosed with lymphangioma and developed an anemic tendency. Some days after surgery to deliver anticancer agents to the affected site, the condition worsened. The tongue became swollen, blocked the airway, and prevented breathing	Asahi E

(continued)

Table 4.1 (continued)

Date	Accident or error / Name of medical institution	Injury or harm	Content of newspaper article (extract)	Source / Classification
2001 Aug.	Injury to colon during examination caused patient death / Niigata Prefectural Koide Hospital (Currently Uonuma City Koide Hospital)	Death of female in 80s	Endoscopic examination in screening for colon cancer was followed by symptoms including fever and septicemia, but the patient's condition improved. However, blood pressure dropped some days later, breathing stopped, and death from heart failure ensued	Asahi / A
2001 Sept. 26	Patient failed to regain consciousness after appendix surgery / Fukushima Prefectural Inawashiro Hospital (Currently Inawashiro Municipal Inawashiro Hospital)	Teenage female remained unconscious for one month	It was discovered that a patient who had undergone appendicitis surgery failed to regain consciousness for one month after surgery. There was thought to have been a mistake in either the anesthetic dose or the administration method	Asahi / A
2001 Oct. 2	Intravenous administration of stomach drug through wrong tube, immediately halted / Kashima Kosei Hospital	Female in 70s. No health damage ensued	Confusion between a tube into the patient's gastrointestinal tract and a tube for intravenous drip infusion. The nurse apparently connected to the port of the drip infusion tube a drug intended to improve digestive function	Asahi / B
2001 Nov. 26	Reoperation to remove surgical instrument left in body / Kasugai Municipal Hospital	67-year-old male. No health damage ensued	During surgery, an instrument for fixing the blood vessel known as a stabilizer was attached to the coronary artery, but suturing was performed with the tip part of the instrument still in the body	Asahi / E
2001 Nov. 30	Bleeding during surgery in heart region due to vein injury / Nakadori General Hospital	Death of 45-year-old male	After surgery to remove a lump in the heart region, the surgeon mistakenly caused injury to a vein resulting in bleeding. The patient fell into a critical condition and died	Asahi / A
2001 Dec. 25	Patient death after anemia was overlooked / Sapporo Medical University Hospital	Death of male in 70s	An intern doctor in the internal medicine department failed to check the result of a blood test and therefore failed to notice severe anemia. The patient shortly after suffered ischemic brain infarction, fell unconscious, and died	Asahi / A
2001 Dec.	Nutrition tube inserted into trachea / University of Tokyo Hospital	Death of male in 50s	A nutrition tube was inserted through the nose. After nutrient infusion, the patient regurgitated the nutrient. Investigation showed that the nutrition tube was inserted into the trachea. The patient's condition worsened and he died	Asahi / E
2002 Jan. 8	Patient hospitalized for 5 days after injection needle inserted too deep / Yamagata Prefectural Shinjo Hospital	5-day hospitalization of male in 50s	During injection of painkiller into the back, the lung was apparently mistakenly injured. The injection needle was 3 cm long, and is thought to have been inserted too deep. It was commented that the patient's physique should have been taken into account	Asahi / A

(continued)

Table 4.1 (continued)

Date	Accident or error / Name of medical institution	Injury or harm	Content of newspaper article (extract)	Source / Classification
2002 Jan. 14	Patient death after mistake with respirator / Otaru General Hospital	Death of 84-year-old female	A nurse forgot to turn on the switch after exchanging the water in an artificial respirator, causing a temporary state of cardiopulmonary arrest. Subsequently the patient suffered drop in blood pressure and pulse rate and other symptoms and died	Asahi / B
2002 Mar. 11	Nutrition tube mistakenly inserted into trachea causing temporary worsening of condition / General Daiyukai Hospital	89-year-old male recovered fully	The patient removed the tube overnight, so the nurse replaced it. Nutritional fluid was given. However, the nurse mistakenly inserted the nutrition tube into the trachea when it was intended for the stomach and the patient required ICU treatment	Asahi / B
2002 Mar. 15	Surgical gauze left in the body / Nagoya Municipal Josai Hospital (Now closed)	Female patient recovered fully	After surgery for womb fibroids and urinary incontinence, X-ray examination showed a foreign object in the abdomen. A gauze sheet approx. 30 cm^2 was removed in reoperation	Asahi / E
2002 Mar. 28	10-fold excess dose of drug was given 8 times in 5 days without being noticed / Care facility in Gifu Prefecture	Death of 48-year-old male	The prescription was for 2 g of aleviatin daily divided into two doses and diluted 10-fold. However, the treating doctor mistakenly issued a regular prescription for undiluted aleviatin, so that a 10-fold concentration was administered 8 times over 5 days	Asahi / A
2002 Mar. 28	Gauze left in abdomen / Niigata Prefectural Shibata Hospital	Female in 40s recovered fully	After womb surgery, diarrhea persisted and abdominal pain set in. To facilitate surgery, gauze had been used to raise position of small intestine and other organs, but the doctor had forgotten to remove it	Asahi / A
2002 Mar. 29	Death due to intubation mistake / Handa City Hospital	Death of 82-year-old female	A nutritional tube that should normally be passed through the nose into the stomach was mistakenly inserted into the trachea by the duty doctor, so that lukewarm water entered the lung via the tube, causing death from acute lung damage	Asahi / A
2002 Apr. 4	Patient death due to breathing tube being attached to outlet port / Asahi General Hospital	Death of male in 70s	When a nurse adjusted the patient's position, the rubber tube supplying air to the artificial respirator became detached. However, the nurse mistakenly reconnected the tube to the 'flow sensor' (air outlet port) and the patient died	Asahi / B
2002 May	Patient death due to treatment mistake / Tokai University Hospital	Death of 19-year-old male	Treatment was given to remove a throat sarcoma by cauterization, but the tip of the silver nitrate instrument snapped, fell into the trachea, and became unretrievable. Doctor immediately reacted by washing out the trachea, but the patient died	Asahi / A

(continued)

Table 4.1 (continued)

Date	Accident or error Name of medical institution	Injury or harm	Content of newspaper article (extract)	Source Classification
2002 Jun. 1	Patient death following mistaken administration Nagahama Red Cross Hospital	Death of 69-year-old male	It is suspected that around half of a potassium chloride preparation which should normally be introduced through a drip infuser was poured into the tube connecting the drip infuser with the patient's body. The patient's condition deteriorated suddenly and he died	Asahi E
2002 Jun. 8	Patient death due to neglect of verbal check leading to drip infusion mistake Kaetsu Hospital	Death of 71-year-old female	A potassium chloride preparation was meant to be mixed in drip infusion bag, but the assistant nurse injected it via syringe not into the drip infusion bag but from part way along the drip infusion tube	Asahi B
2002 Aug. 12	Patient death from post-surgical measures: 'unavoidable accident' Yokohama City University Medical Center	Death of female in 70s	To clear bodily fluids, etc., that had collected in the thoracic cavity after surgery, an attempt was made to insert a tube leading upwards from the chest along the lung. However, as there was adhesion between the lung and the chest wall, injury and bleeding were caused to the pulmonary artery and other tissues and death resulted from multi-organ failure	Asahi A
2002 Aug. 12	Patient bled to death during womb cancer surgery Reported as medical accident National Cancer Center Hospital	Death of 47-year-old female	Hysterectomy was performed. As there was a risk of cancer spread to the lymph nodes, pelvic lymph nodes were removed, leading to heavy bleeding and patient death of heart failure	Asahi E
2002 Aug. 16	Drug introduced into wrong tube Mutsu General Hospital	Death of 63-year-old female	An antidiarrhea medication which should have been given via a tube from the nose to the duodenum was mistakenly inserted by the nurse into a tube from the collar bone to a blood vessel	Asahi B
2002 Aug.	Death of male 1 week after mistake in order of administration of anticancer agents Noda Municipal Hospital	Death of 64-year-old male	The patient was given two different anticancer agents in the wrong order and died 1 week later. The hospital acknowledged the mistake, but claimed that it was not the cause of death	Asahi E
2002 Sept. 9	Patient death from heart failure following possible mistake in heart surgery Dokkyo Medical University Hospital	Death of 74-year-old male	Surgery was performed on a ventricular septal defect which consisted of covering the hole with artificial fabric, but cardiopulmonary function deteriorated and death ensued. Inques showed that the fabric covering the hole had blocked the blood flow	Asahi A
2002 Sept. 25	Inoculation of expired vaccine Koka Municipal Hospital	18-month old boy and 16-month-old girl. No health damage	Measles vaccine was distributed by the municipality. Up till the expiry date, 27 of the 30 lots had been used, but the remaining vaccine was left in the cool store of the hospital pharmacy	Asahi D

(continued)

Table 4.1 (continued)

Date	Accident or error / Name of medical institution	Injury or harm	Content of newspaper article (extract)	Source / Classification
2002 Oct. 21	Misoperation of instrument during examination / Nakatsu Municipal Hospital	45-year-old female patient discharged from hospital	After heart catheter examination, air was mistakenly introduced into a blood vessel. This was noticed during the procedure and aspiration was immediately applied but the patient fell unconscious and a cerebral thrombus occurred. The patient was treated at another hospital and was discharged	Asahi / A
2002 Nov.	Amaryl was prescribed instead of the intended almarl and patient suffered disturbed consciousness / Private hospital in Osaka Prefecture	85-year-old female suffered disturbed consciousness	Instead of the antihypertensive drug almarl, which reduces hand tremor, the antidiabetic drug amaryl was mistakenly prescribed, and the patient suffered two hypoglycemic attacks and disturbed consciousness	Asahi / A
2002 Dec.	Patient death due to drug administration mistake, with injection of drug at fivefold concentration / Hirosaki University Hospital	Death of male in 70s	The patient condition worsened after surgery and arrhythmia appeared. An antiarrhythmic agent should have been administered at a concentration of 2%, but was mistakenly injected intravenously at a concentration of 10%. The patient suffered cardiopulmonary arrest and died	Asahi / A
2003 Jan. 7	Patient death through excess administration of anticancer agent / National Defense Medical College Hospital	Death of male in 60s	During treatment with anticancer agents, the patient was supposed to receive continuous administration for 5 days then repeated administration after a 3-week break, but it is suspected that the attending physicians left only a 2-day break, resulting in excessive administration	Mainichi / E
2003 Jan. 15	Patient death due to dialysis mistake in which artery was intubated without hemostasis / Nagoya City University Hospital	Death of female in 70s from hemorrhagic shock	Condition of patient who had artificial dialysis deteriorated suddenly, and she died the next day. The hospital acknowledged the strong possibility of medical error in which, during dialysis, hemostasis failed after the tube was inserted into the wrong blood vessel	Mainichi / A
2003 Jan. 17	Patient death during pre-surgical anesthesia due to tube mistakenly inserted into esophagus / Matsue Red Cross Hospital	Death of male in 50s	To secure breathing during general anesthesia prior to lung resection, the anesthesiologist inserted a tube through the mouth into the trachea. However, after changing the patient's position, the anesthesiologist mistakenly replaced the tube in the esophagus	Mainichi / A
2003 Jan. 20	Patient injured in accident had eyelid stitched without removing fragment of tooth / Kitakyushu Municipal Emergency Medical Center	19-year-old female	The patient went to a clinic after colliding with the bicycle of a high-school student and cutting the left eyelid. The next day, during restitching at the plastic surgery clinic, several tooth fragments of several millimeters in length were retrieved from the wound	Mainichi / A

(continued)

Table 4.1 (continued)

Date	Accident or error / Name of medical institution	Injury or harm	Content of newspaper article (extract)	Source / Classification
2003 Jan. 22	Injury to aorta during hernia surgery / Sanin Rosai Hospital	Death of 37-year-old female due to heavy bleeding	The patient was hospitalized on Day 14 and had surgery on Day 22. According to the hospital, the surgeon (43) mistakenly injured the abdominal aorta when removing the hernia	Mainichi / A
2003 Jan. 27	Patient death due to needle coming loose during artificial dialysis / Haibara General Hospital	Death of male in 80s	During artificial dialysis, a needle in the arm came loose and the patient began bleeding and died of cardiopulmonary arrest the same day. The hospital had left the patient alone for approx. 30 min during dialysis	Mainichi / C
2003 Jan. 28	Inattention caused accidental death by fall / Private clinic in Tono City, Iwate Prefecture	Death of 68-year-old male	To help the patient to the toilet, the nurse removed the safety rail from the bed, but while she was not looking he fell. No obvious injury occurred, but during artificial dialysis, blood pressure fell and the patient died	Mainichi / C
2003 Jan.	Mistake in treatment of victim, transfusion not possible due to procedural mistake / Gunma University Hospital	Patient death	Patient was in cardiac arrest, but showed response to electrocardiogram, following heart massage, etc. Preparation therefore began for urgent transfusion, but the doctor misjudged type B as type AB in a blood type test, and transfusion was not possible	Mainichi / F
2003 Feb. 13	Mistake in attachment of tube / Kyushu University Hospital	Death of male in 80s from heart failure	When the nurse administered the drug, a T-shaped connecting tube with a hole for expelling breath should have been attached to the tube, but by mistake an L-shaped tube with no hole was used	Mainichi / B
2003 Feb. 19	Treatment drug administered at 100-fold concentration / Tohoku University Hospital	Temporary loss of consciousness in male minor	The hospital diagnosed theophylline poisoning from test results, etc. Based on investigation of the cause, the prescription should have ordered 100-fold dilution of the drug, but the pharmacist mistakenly prepared it without dilution	Mainichi / D
2003 Mar. 4	During leukemia examination, needle damaged heart / Tokyo Medical University Hospital	Death of 76-year-old male	A former internal medicine specialist suspected leukemia and injected a needle into the breastbone to sample bone marrow fluid, but the needle passed through the bone and damaged the heart, and the patient suffered cardiac arrest immediately after. Suspected death from septicemia	Mainichi / A
2003 Mar.	Temporary cardiac arrest and deterioration of lung function due to misoperation of transfusion pump / Osaka University Hospital	Possibility of patient suffering sequelae	In transfusion during surgery, although the transfusion tube was detached part way through the procedure, the pump was not turned off, so that air entered through the tube, bloodflow deteriorated, and the heart stopped	Mainichi / E

(continued)

Table 4.1 (continued)

Date	Accident or error Name of medical institution	Injury or harm	Content of newspaper article (extract)	Source Classification
2003 Apr. 7	Patient death 5 weeks after transfusion mistake in lung cancer surgery Nemuro City Hospital	Death of 81-year-old male from pulmonary edema	During surgery, a blood transfusion of type B was mistakenly given to a patient of type A. The hospital noticed the mistake and transferred the patient to the ICU for emergency treatment, but he died on May 14 of pulmonary edema	Mainichi F
2003 Apr. 9	Sequelae due to drug administration mistake Aomori City Hospital	Severe sequelae in male neonate	A drug administration mistake was made in CT examination, leaving severe sequelae. The CT examination was for a suspected condition in which urine accumulates in the kidney	Mainichi D
2003 Apr. 30	Hospital patient death from intestinal necrosis after failure to notice artery blockage Taga General Hospital	Death of 59-year-old female	The patient was hospitalized for rehabilitation after cerebral infarction. The abdominal artery was blocked and the patient complained of abdominal pain, but the doctor failed to notice the arterial blockage, and the patient died 3 days later	Yomiuri A
2003 Apr.	Incision made at wrong site in artificial inner ear surgery due to left-right confusion Tokyo Medical University Hospital	Surgery on wrong site in infant	In surgery to implant an artificial inner ear, the left and right ears were confused and an incision made at the wrong site. Two consecutive artificial inner ear implants were scheduled for the same day, and the nurse had confused the patients and mistakenly prepared for surgery on the wrong ear	Mainichi B
2003 May	Fetal death due to drug side-effect PMDA	Fetal death from drug side-effect	Fetus died due to drug side-effect. Near to the due date, a hormonal agent was administered to dilate the mouth of the womb, shortly after which the fetus was stillborn	Mainichi D
2003 May	Gauze left in body Iwaki Kyoritsu Hospital	66-year-old female. No sequelae	The patient had surgery to resect womb cancer and was discharged in June, but lost her appetite and had persistent fever so was readmitted in July for examination. Gauze was found to have been left in the body and reoperation took place	Mainichi E
2003 Jun. 15	Patient death after delayed surgery following failure to notice 'hole in colon' in CT examination Oyama City Hospital (Currently Shin-Oyama City Hospital)	Death of 71-year-old female from peritonitis	In CT examination, two internal medicine specialists diagnosed intestinal blockage, but the patient was found to have a colonic perforation of unknown cause. Urgent surgery and treatment continued, but the patient developed comorbid peritonitis on the afternoon of the 17th and died	Mainichi E

(continued)

Table 4.1 (continued)

Date	Accident or error Name of medical institution	Injury or harm	Content of newspaper article (extract)	Source Classification
2003 Jun.	After pneumonia diagnosis, transfer to specialist hospital was delayed. Chiba Tarumi Hospital	Death of 53-year-old male due to airway occlusion	The patient had fever and chest X-ray showed lung inflammation. He was diagnosed at another hospital with mild pneumonia but his condition changed suddenly and he fell into cardiopulmonary arrest. He was transferred but died	Mainichi A
2003 Jun.	Death from pharyngeal bleeding due to excessive dose of radiation Wakayama Medical University Hospital	Death of 70-year-old male from pharyngeal bleeding	A patient with pharyngeal cancer received an excessive dose of radiation and died of pharyngeal bleeding. The patient had been hospitalized with early-stage cancer and was being treated with drug administration and radiation	Mainichi A
2003 Jun.	Death from bleeding in Cesarean section Iwaki Kyoritsu Hospital	Death of 32-year-old female from major bleeding	The patient was hospitalized for pregnancy toxemia and the delivery was made by Cesarean section in line with the doctor's instructions. However, bleeding persisted and the patient died of major hemorrhage	Mainichi A
2003 Jul. 31	Patient with hydrocephalus died due to surgical mistake Fukuoka Hakuiyuji Hospital	Death of 52-year-old female from hemorrhagic shock	Two doctors drilled a hole in the skull, but are suspected of having failed to take the mandatory precaution of making marks to confirm the position and damaged a venous sinus at the back of the head, causing death from hemorrhagic shock	Mainichi E
2003 Jul.	Death of artificial dialysis patient from 'unknown cause' Showa Inan General Hospital	Death of male in 40s, female in 50s in serious condition	One patient died in artificial dialysis and another fell into a serious condition. The male in his 40s suffered an abnormal drop in platelet level with accompanying liver dysfunction. As the female in her 50s had similar symptoms, the artificial dialysis machine was thought to be the cause	Mainichi A
2003 Jul.	Inexperienced surgeon changed surgical approach during operation but was unable to halt bleeding Yokohama Cerebrovascular Medicine Center	Female in 50s fell unconscious	The patient fell into serious consciousness disturbance due to a medical error by the surgeon and others. A male doctor with no experience of endoscopic surgery on females was in charge. During the procedure he changed the approach to craniotomy, but bleeding persisted and the patient fell unconscious	Mainichi G
2003 Aug. 6	Patient death after breathing accidentally blocked during oxygen supply Chimeido Hospital	Death of 87-year-old female	A nurse inserted a tube to supply oxygen into a catheter and fixed the catheter to the mouth with an adhesive plaster, but it was mistakenly set up in a way that blocked breathing	Mainichi B

(continued)

Table 4.1 (continued)

Date	Accident or error / Name of medical institution	Injury or harm	Content of newspaper article (extract)	Source / Classification
2003 Aug.	Neglect of treatment after birth / Kuroishi General Hospital	Infant suffered severe damage	Immediately after birth, the infant was in a state of apparent death, but instead of immediately contacting a pediatrician, no measures were taken until convulsions began. As a result the patient was diagnosed with cerebral palsy due to hypoxemic-ischemic brain damage and suffered severe damage	Mainichi / G
2003 Aug.	Patient death following drug administration mistake / Kobe University Hospital	Death of female in 60s	Mistake in drug administration to female hospital patient. The patient was hospitalized for an infectious disease due to esophageal perforation, but instead of anticoagulant heparin, insulin for diabetes was mistakenly administered so that blood sugar levels rose to three times normal and the patient died	Mainichi / D
2003 Sept. 1	Patient in serious condition due to transfusion mistake / University of Tokyo Hospital	Female in 20s fell into serious state of unconsciousness	During urgent liver surgery, a valve on the pipe supplying transfusion fluid to the transfusion pump was not sufficiently shut off, so that when the transfusion volume was raised, air entered through the gap, causing arrhythmia and temporary cardiac arrest	Mainichi / E
2003 Sept. 3	Patient death following reoperation after failure to remove a blood-absorbing swab from the head / Nagano National Hospital Neurosurgery Department (Currently National Hospital Organization Shinshu Ueda Medical Center)	Death of 15-year-old junior high-school pupil	In surgery to remove brain abscess from junior high-school pupil, a blood-absorbing swab was left behind inside the head, and when general anesthesia was introduced for reoperation, the heart went into temporary arrest. The patient died 11 days later without regaining consciousness	Mainichi / E
2003 Sept. 14	Urgent measures neglected after breathing difficulties during local anesthesia / Private hospital	Death of female in 50s from pneumonia	During facial surgery, local anesthesia was applied around the patient's face, but the airway became blocked approx. 3 h later and breathing difficulties developed. It is suspected that the doctor nevertheless failed to introduce pressurized oxygen supply and other necessary urgent measures	Mainichi / A
2003 Sept. 17	Death morning after diagnosis of 'no abnormality,' possible failure to notice lung contusion / Ohda Municipal Hospital	Death of male in 60s	A patient hospitalized after a traffic accident was conscious, received treatment at the hospital, and was judged to have no abnormality in the chest, etc., but the next morning his family found him collapsed on the toilet	Mainichi / A
2003 Sept.	Patient death in radiation treatment due mainly to excessive irradiation / Wakayama Medical University Hospital	Death of male in 70s	A pharyngeal cancer patient exposed to excessive radiation choked to death due to pharyngeal bleeding. The radiation specialist and the engineer twice mistakenly delivered four times the planned dose	Mainichi / E

(continued)

Table 4.1 (continued)

Date	Accident or error Name of medical institution	Injury or harm	Content of newspaper article (extract)	Source Classification
2003 Sept.	Patient death during retransfer to hospital after misdiagnosis Mie Prefectural General Medical Center	Death of male in 50s	The patient complained of abdominal pain and an intern doctor and the digestive medicine specialist diagnosed urinary tract stones, but examination at another hospital gave a diagnosis of rupture of abdominal aortic aneurysm. The patient died of cardiac arrest	Mainichi E
2003 Sept.	Death due to administration of wrong anticancer agent Kagoshima University Hospital	Death of male in 60s from multi-organ failure	The patient died after administration of anticancer agents of a different type to that intended. The intern doctor made a mis-entry on the computerized prescription note	Mainichi F
2003 Oct. 17	Patient fell unconscious after administration of liver reagent Jichi Medical University Hospital	Male in 50s fell unconscious	For liver examination, 30 mg of the medical reagent indocyanine green was injected into the vein, provoking a serious allergic reaction including breathing difficulties and consciousness disturbance	Mainichi F
2003 Oct. 21	Persistent damage after failure to notice dislocation Haramachi Municipal Hospital (Currently Minamisoma City General Hospital)	Female child left with damage to left elbow	A part-time male doctor who examined the child for the first time diagnosed sprain. Another doctor, an orthopedic surgeon, saw the patient on a visit to the hospital on Dec. 3, 2003, and diagnosed dislocation of the left radial head, which is the exterior bone	Mainichi A
2003 Oct. 26	Patient death after delay in transfer following diagnosis Warabi City Hospital	Death of 67-year-old male	After complaining of abdominal pain and being hospitalized by ambulance, the patient was diagnosed with intestinal blockage and transferred 10 h later for urgent surgery to Kawaguchi Municipal Medical Center, but died the next day	Mainichi H
2003 Oct.	Cardiotonic drug administered at 10-fold concentration due to mistake Hyogo Prefectural Amagasaki Hospital	Death of 5-month-old male infant	Infant with heart disease was mistakenly given a cardiotonic drug at 10-fold concentration and died. The report identified the cause of death as acute-drug poisoning through mis-administration	Mainichi D
2003 Nov. 5	Mistake during tube insertion for patient examination led to injury to blood vessel and removal of kidney Shizuoka City Shizuoka Hospital	58-year-old male had the left kidney removed	To investigate blood flow in a blood vessel in the heart region, a catheter of 3 mm diameter was inserted via an artery at the top of the right leg, but mistakenly entered a blood vessel connecting to the kidney, causing injury to the blood vessel	Mainichi A
2003 Nov. 12	Nitrogen mistakenly used for respiration instead of oxygen Yokohama City University Medical Center	3-month-old male child suffered temporary respiratory arrest	Infant hospitalized for surgery for premature retinopathy was mistakenly given nitrogen instead of oxygen. The patient suffered temporary respiratory arrest but is now stable	Mainichi E

(continued)

Table 4.1 (continued)

Date	Accident or error Name of medical institution	Injury or harm	Content of newspaper article (extract)	Source Classification
2003 Nov. 15	Death following mistaken drug administration Matsugasaki Memorial Hospital	Death of 73-year-old male from acute poisoning	After patient suffered a sudden change of condition, the intention was to give an injection of 5 ml of lidocaine hydrochloride 2% solution to prevent arrhythmia, but instead 10 ml of a 10% solution was mistakenly given by drip infusion	Mainichi D
2003 Nov. 18	Artery damaged during endoscopic surgery Kyoto University Hospital	Death of 63-year-old female	During surgery, use was made of a thoracoscope, a type of endoscope which allows body parts to be examined by camera from outside the body. The hospital acknowledged the strong possibility that the aorta was mistakenly damaged	Mainichi A
2003 Nov. 19	Laparoscopy accident caused by mistake in technical management Fukushima Prefectural Inawashiro Hospital (Currently Inawashiro Municipal Inawashiro Hospital)	Death of 67-year-old male from multi-organ failure	During laparoscopic surgery, the doctor mistakenly severed an artery and therefore switched to laparotomy to control bleeding and resected the gall bladder, but the patient died of multi-organ failure caused by hemorrhagic shock	Mainichi A
2003 Nov. 20	Mistaken administration of hypoglycemic drug led to temporary unconsciousness in male on artificial dialysis Yamagata Prefectural Kahoku Hospital	Male in 50s fell temporarily unconscious	Instead of the antihypertensive almarl, the hypoglycemic drug amaryl was mistakenly given. The patient took amaryl at home, and on the 24th blood sugar levels fell to approx. one quarter of normal and he fell unconscious	Mainichi D
2003 Nov. 21	Accident in blood vessel surgery to treat cerebral artery aneurysm, damage possibly caused by catheter St. Luke's International Hospital	55-year-old male fell into serious unconscious state	An unsuccessful attempt to mend the aneurysm with a coil was made, and the catheter had to be removed. Blood vessel imaging immediately after showed subarachnoid bleeding and surgery was discontinued	Mainichi A
2003 Nov. 30	Mistake in insertion of catheter caused injury to artery Kawasaki Municipal Hospital	Death of 70-year-old female from multi-organ failure	During insertion of a catheter for surgery to examine the heart and widen a blood vessel, mishandling caused injury to an artery close to the small intestine, leading to multi-organ failure due to hemorrhagic shock. The patient died some days later	Mainichi A
2003 Nov.	Death of 94-year-old arrhythmia patient in catheter treatment Private general hospital in Kita Ward, Osaka	Death of 94-year-old male from heart rupture	Sudden patient death from heart rupture occurred during arrhythmia treatment, suspected that the catheter opened a hole in the heart. The hospital had not clearly explained to the patient the risk of death due to heart rupture	Mainichi A

(continued)

Table 4.1 (continued)

Date	Accident or error Name of medical institution	Injury or harm	Content of newspaper article (extract)	Source Classification
2003 Dec. 12	Detachment of artificial respirator tube Watari Hospital	Death of 67-year-old male from multi-organ failure	The patient was hospitalized for chronic bronchitis. The abnormality alarm of the artificial respirator sounded and the nurse rushed to the ward to find the fixing tape had come loose and the tube detached	Mainichi C
2003 Dec. 15	Doctor caused injury to artery with needle Uwajima City Hospital	Death of male in 70s	An examination was carried out in which a needle was inserted into the breastbone to collect bone marrow fluid, but partly because the disease had softened the bone, the needle passed through the bone and injured the artery	Mainichi A
2003 Dec.	Aggravation of drug-induced pneumonia through mistake in drug administration Tokyo-to Shokuin Kyosai-kumiai Aoyama Hospital (Now closed)	Male patient left with sequelae to respiratory organs	During treatment for nail disease, the patient developed drug-induced pneumonia which was aggravated by a drug administration mistake, leaving sequelae for the respiratory organs. An internal medicine specialist had diagnosed another form of pneumonia and continued antibiotics at an increased dose, thus aggravating the drug-induced pneumonia	Mainichi D
2003 Dec.	Nutrient introduced into abdominal cavity Shiga University of Medical Science Hospital	Female in 40s fell into comatose state	A tube for draining blood, ascites, etc., from the abdominal cavity was confused with a nutrient tube. A night-shift nurse mistakenly introduced nutrient	Mainichi B
2004 Jan. 31	Injury to artery by catheter Tokyo Medical University Hospital	Female in 60s suffered temporary cardiac arrest	An internal medicine specialist injected a needle to insert a catheter from under the right collarbone, but injured an artery and caused bleeding. The blood compressed the trachea and caused breathing difficulties and temporary cardiac arrest	Mainichi A
2004 Jan. 31	Patient fell unconscious after breathing tube became detached Kyorin University Hospital	2-year-old male child suffered severe brain damage	A nurse who checked on the ward discovered the patient's breathing tube had become detached and the patient was in cardiopulmonary arrest. In subsequent treatment the patient was revived but did not regain consciousness	Mainichi C
2004 Feb. 17	Sudden death following pacemaker implant Kawasaki Municipal Ida Hospital	Death of female in 70s	After surgery to implant a cardiac pacemaker, the patient condition worsened and she died. A blood vessel in the neck was injured and she asphyxiated	Mainichi A
2004 Feb. 25	Death of hospital patient after combined use of prohibited anticancer agents St. Marianna University School of Medicine, Toyoko Hospital	Death of male in 60s from multi-organ failure	A patient hospitalized for colon cancer treatment was simultaneously prescribed two oral anticancer agents whose concurrent use is prohibited and died of multi-organ failure	Mainichi D

(continued)

Table 4.1 (continued)

Date	Accident or error / Name of medical institution	Injury or harm	Content of newspaper article (extract)	Source / Classification
2004 Feb.	Attending physician misinterpreted image / Fukushima Prefectural Miyashita Hospital	Death of female in 70s from acute circulatory failure	For surgery, a tube was attached to drain bile, but due to force being applied during suture, the tube became detached and the bile spread through the body. Given the additional inadequate management of breathing, the patient died of acute circulatory failure	Mainichi / E
2004 Mar. 20	Accident during treatment left patient in temporary serious condition / Okayama University Hospital	Female in 70s became temporarily unconscious	During radiofrequency ablation of a tumor at a site adjacent to the heart, a needle injection mistakenly pierced the pouch-like membrane covering the heart. The gathering blood caused cardiac tamponade leading to circulatory insufficiency	Mainichi / A
2004 Mar. 23	Electrocardiogram alarm was ignored 20 times, resulting in death of student with heart disease / Sakakibara Heart Institute	Death of 23-year-old male	The electrocardiogram monitor screen of a patient hospitalized for heart disease showed abnormality and the alarm sounded but was ignored for over 1 h and the patient died. At the time, the system did not allow for a nurse to be constantly in attendance at the nurse station	Mainichi / G
2004 Mar.	Tube mispositioned during replacement, resulting in inflammation / Yokohama Cerebrovascular Medicine Center	Patient in 60s suffered inflammation	During the exchange of the nutrient tube of a patient hospitalized for stroke, the tube was mispositioned. leading to inflammation	Mainichi / A
2004 Apr. 6	Intern doctor failed to check dose / Kitasato University Hospital	Death of 76-year-old female from lidocaine poisoning	The patient was given an intravenous injection of 20 times the required dose, fell into cardiac arrest 3 min later, and died of lidocaine poisoning at 00:46 on the morning of the 7th	Mainichi / D
2004 Apr. 22	Patient death due to tube becoming detached / Yokohama Rosai Hospital	Death of female in 60s due to hypoxic-ischemic encephalopathy	When two nurses changed the position of a female patient, a tube in the trachea became dislodged and was refixed, but immediately afterwards blood oxygen levels fell and the patient died on the morning of the 30th	Mainichi / B
2004 Apr.	Injury to rectum during surgical disinfection resulted in postoperative peritonitis / Obama Public Hospital (Currently Sugita Genpaku Memorial Obama Municipal Hospital)	Death of female in 70s	The patient suffered injury to the rectum during disinfection for rectal surgery, but the doctors failed to notice and continued with the surgery. The patient developed peritonitis postoperatively and was reoperated but died 3 days later	Mainichi / E
2004 May 12	Patient death due to mistake with drip infusion / Kinugasa Hospital	Death of 86-year-old female	A nurse following instructions from the duty doctor mistook a drip-infused antiarrhythmic agent for an intravenous antiarrhythmic agent and mistakenly injected it into the vein. leading to immediate death of the patient	Mainichi / B

(continued)

Table 4.1 (continued)

Date	Accident or error / Name of medical institution	Injury or harm	Content of newspaper article (extract)	Source / Classification
2004 May 15	Patient death following undiluted drug administration. Investigation on suspicion of corporate manslaughter / Japanese Red Cross Narita Hospital	Death of female in 60s from heart failure	Doctor gave instructions for a drip infusion pack containing nutrient to be administered after admixture of potassium chloride preparation, but the nurse used a syringe to introduce the preparation via the port of the drip infusion tube, resulting in patient death	Mainichi / B
2004 May 16	Use of the lid of a blood sampling tube, which 'was used routinely as a replacement' / Kyoto City Hospital	Male in 50s fell into serious state of unconsciousness	A nurse made a mistake in the handling of a tracheotomy tube. It was found that the wrongly attached lid was that of a blood sampling tube. Possible that the nurse may have confused the tube types	Mainichi / B
2004 May 26	Temporarily reduced consciousness after air entered heart lung machine / Tottori University Hospital	Temporarily reduced patient consciousness	During treatment of a heart disease patient, the anesthesiologist mistakenly allowed air to enter the artificial heart lung machine, causing temporarily reduced patient consciousness	Mainichi / A
2004 Jun. 19	Excessive dose of radiation / Wakayama Medical University Hospital	Death of male from pharyngeal bleeding	The patient was mistakenly given 4 times the intended dose of radiation and died on May 9th of pharyngeal bleeding	Mainichi / E
2004 Jun.	Abnormality overlooked on CT scan, patient died of subarachnoid bleeding / Gifu University Hospital	Death of female in 30s	The patient was admitted to the hospital's advanced critical care center with symptoms including headache and numbness in the left arm. Due to delayed discovery of subarachnoid bleeding, the patient died approx. 1 month later	Mainichi / F
2004 Jul. 29	Patient death due to fault with medical instrument / Iwate Prefectural Kitakami Hospital	Death of male in 40s	Patient died after a catheter inserted during coronary artery angioplasty became impossible to remove. Possible that a fault in the medical instrument was the cause	Mainichi / H
2004 Jul.	During gallstone surgery, medical sponge was left in body / Kinan Hospital	No health damage occurred	During gallstone surgery on a male patient, a medical sponge (diameter 5 cm, length 10 cm) was left in the body. This was discovered in postoperative X-ray examination and removed 1 week later	Mainichi / E
2004 Aug. 10	Hole formed in small intestine during radiofrequency treatment / Osaka General Medical Center	Death of male in 60s from multi-organ failure	The patient, a former doctor, who received treatment to remove liver cancer cells with radiofrequency, suffered perforation of the small intestine, developed peritonitis and other symptoms, and died 3 months later	Mainichi / A
2004 Aug. 19	Patient death after tube wrongly inserted into lung / Kanagawa Prefectural Ashigarakami Hospital	Death of 84-year-old male from acute pneumonia	The patient died after a tube was mistakenly inserted into the lung	Mainichi / E

(continued)

Table 4.1 (continued)

Date	Accident or error Name of medical institution	Injury or harm	Content of newspaper article (extract)	Source Classification
2004 Aug.	Hole in small intestine caused by 'chance accident' Osaka General Medical Center	Death of male in 60s	After receiving surgery to remove liver cancer cells by radiofrequency, the patient died due to a hole in the small intestine. Due to the patient's body moving unexpectedly, the tip of the electrode needle apparently moved and caused the hole	Mainichi C
2004 Aug.	Fall from wheeled stretcher Fukushima Prefectural Miyashita Hospital	53-year-old female suffered bruising to lower back requiring 3 weeks' treatment	A patient who had been treated for lower back issue tried to sit up while on a wheeled stretcher, the stretcher moved, and she suffered bruising to the lower back requiring 3 weeks' treatment. The stretcher's safety mechanism was imperfect	Mainichi C
2004 Sept. 21	Patient death through mistaken insertion of stomach tube into lung Nagamachi Hospital Clinic	Death of female in 80s from pneumonia	A patient whose nutrient stomach tube had been changed suffered a sudden change in condition and died. The tube had been inserted into the lung instead of the stomach. Nurse had not adequately followed procedure when changing tube	Mainichi B
2004 Sept. 22	Patient death due to mistake in artificial respirator device. The alarm was switched off and left for 13 min Kikuna Memorial Hospital	Death of 73-year-old male	A mistake in the artificial respirator device prevented oxygen supply for 13 min, leading to patient death	Mainichi E
2004 Sept.	Drill entered brain during surgery causing unilateral paralysis Handa City Hospital	Male in 70s left with left-side paralysis	The patient was diagnosed with chronic subdural hematoma. When the drill was used to make a hole in the skull in neurological surgery, it mistakenly entered the brain, leaving unilateral paralysis and other damage	Mainichi A
2004 Oct. 18	Patient death after surgeon injured vein JR Sendai Hospital	Death of 70-year-old female from hemorrhagic shock	In laparotomy to remove intestinal blockage, there was adhesion between the affected site and the pelvis, which the surgeon tried to separate with a scissors, but the vein suffered injury and the patient died of hemorrhagic shock	Mainichi A
2004 Oct. 25	Excessive drug administration, inadequacies in drug management system, etc. Kyoto University Hospital	Death of male in 70s from respiratory failure	Medical error involving excessive administration of the rheumatoid arthritis drug Rheumatrex. Infringement of the rules on the drug's prescription method. etc., and inadequate check system	Mainichi D
2004 Nov.	Patient death after oversight by intern doctor, fault with organization not individual Kochi Prefectural Aki Hospital	Death of male in 80s	A duty intern doctor examining a patient who complained of chest and back pain failed to notice a dissecting aortic aneurysm and sent the patient home. The patient's condition later deteriorated and he died	Mainichi G

(continued)

Table 4.1 (continued)

Date	Accident or error / Name of medical institution	Injury or harm	Content of newspaper article (extract)	Source / Classification
2004 Dec. 8	Rubber part left after laparotomy / Nara Prefectural Nara Hospital (Currently Nara Prefecture General Medical Center)	Female in 70s / No sequelae	A rubber part of a medical instrument was left in the body after laparotomy. The mistake was discovered in X-ray examination and it was removed in reoperation 2 days later	Mainichi / E
2004 Dec. 17	Intestinal cleaning tube and connector left in body / Secomedic Hospital	Death of 85-year-old male from multi-organ failure	A patient with cerebral contusion underwent endoscopic examination and died afterward. An intestinal cleaning tube and its plastic connector were left behind in the intestine	Mainichi / E
2004 Dec.	Patient death during drip infusion due to failure to check allergy / Osaka Prefectural Lifestyle Related Disease Center (Currently Osaka International Cancer Center)	Death of male in 60s	A patient with allergy to pirin-type drugs was given an antifebrile drug containing the same constituent and died. The allergy was recorded in the medical notes, but the attending physician and nurse failed to check before giving drip infusion	Mainichi / F
2005 Jan. 11	Patient had gauze left in abdomen after surgery / Hachinohe City Hospital	Female in 40s. No danger to life	The patient had surgery on the womb and ovaries, but a 25 cm^2 piece of gauze used for hemostasis was left rolled up inside the body	Mainichi / E
2005 Jan. 26	Vaccine past expiry date was given to prevent rubella / Medical institution in Saku area of Nagano	19-month-old infant suffered no health damage	In preventive inoculation, the vaccine expiry date and other details are checked, but in this case the check was neglected and the inoculation was mistakenly given to the infant without noticing that it was past its expiry date	Mainichi / D
2005 Jan.	Mistaken administration to artificial dialysis patient of drug which should not have been given / Ōdate Municipal General Hospital	Patient death	An arrhythmia drug not suited to artificial dialysis patients was mistakenly administered by internal medicine specialist and patient died	Mainichi / D
2005 Jan.	Injury to wall of womb and intestine during surgery / Yokohama Municipal Citizen's Hospital	Female in 30s made full recovery	A patient who experienced irregular bleeding after leaving hospital following childbirth was given urgent surgery by a female doctor and suffered accidental injury to the wall of the womb and the intestine	Mainichi / A
2005 Feb.	Patient with osteoporosis suffered fracture of arm and both legs / Nagano Children's Hospital	8-year-old girl suffered three fractures	A patient hospitalized for acute pneumonia suffered fractures in three places during the treatment process. It was explained that the hospital exercised insufficient care assessment toward the patient, who had osteoporosis	Mainichi / F

(continued)

Table 4.1 (continued)

Date	Accident or error / Name of medical institution	Injury or harm	Content of newspaper article (extract)	Source / Classification
2005 Mar. 31	Patient death when nutrient was fed into lung due to misinsertion of tube / Chiba Cerebral and Cardiovascular Center	Death of female in 70s	The patient's nutrition tube was mistakenly inserted into the trachea by a nurse so that nutrient entered the lung and caused death	Mainichi / B
2005 Mar.	Consciousness disturbance caused by excessive drug administration / Nabari City Hospital	71-year-old male fell into vegetative state	Due to excessive dose of hypnotic sedative, the patient suffered consciousness disturbance. The patient was hospitalized with suspected common bile duct stone. The hypnotic sedative was injected for endoscopic examination to ensure that the patient did not suffer injury to the digestive tract due to sudden movement	Mainichi / D
2005 Apr. 2	Death of 4 patients undergoing heart valve surgery / Tokyo Medical University Hospital	Death of 4 patients	Four patients died undergoing heart valve surgery. An investigative committee of outside specialists concluded the cause to be chiefly 'basic insufficiency of knowledge and skills of operating doctor' and recognized the incident as an accident	Mainichi / A
2005 Apr. 14	Patient death due to detached respirator tube / Miki City Hospital	Death of 85-year-old male	An artificial respirator tube became detached from the connection port of the machine, and the alarm sounded. The doctor revived the patient with heart massage, but he did not regain consciousness and died on the 19th	Mainichi / G
2005 Apr. 15	Suppository mistakenly prescribed to child, 3 pharmacists failed to spot mistake / Yamanashi Prefectural Central Hospital	5-year-old female child suffered no health damage	A child who should have been prescribed a liquid oral antinausea medicine was mistakenly prescribed a suppository. All 3 duty pharmacists failed to notice the mistake. As the child's mother noticed, the drug was not administered	Mainichi / D
2005 Apr. 18	During drip infusion, needle was inserted into artery. Hemostasis was also inadequate and the patient bled to death / Kikuna Memorial Hospital	Death of patient in 70s	When a male doctor from the internal medicine department was fitting a drip infusion catheter to a hospital patient, he mistakenly inserted the needle into an artery instead of a vein. The resulting injury caused major bleeding, and the patient died of symptoms interpreted as hemorrhagic shock	Mainichi / A
2005 Apr. 22	Excessive dose of drug due to 'mistake by inexperienced doctor' / Asahikawa Medical University Hospital	Death of 80-year-old male from septicemia	The patient was given low-molecular heparin to prevent blood clots, but on the next day, the 23rd, he developed poisoning symptoms and died of septicemia. It was found that the drug had been administered at 5.4 times the normal dose in relation to body weight	Mainichi / D

(continued)

Table 4.1 (continued)

Date	Accident or error Name of medical institution	Injury or harm	Content of newspaper article (extract)	Source Classification
2005 May 12	Inoculation with expired rubella vaccine Hospital in Yatsushiro City, Kumamoto	3-year-old girl suffered no health damage	The nurse failed to check the expiry date before preparing the vaccine and the doctor also did not check at the time of inoculation, so that 0.5 ml of expired vaccine was given	Mainichi D
2005 May 17	Expired oral polio vaccine given to 16 infants Handa City Hospital	16 infants suffered no health damage	Oral polio vaccine past its expiry date was given to 16 infants. The hospital apologized by telephone, etc., to the families	Mainichi D
2005 May 18	Expired vaccine given mistakenly to 11 patients Ibaraki Prefecture Chikusei Health Care Center	11 males and females aged 3–30 years old suffered no health damage	The patients were mistakenly given preventive inoculation of expired polio vaccine. The duty staff member apparently forgot to check the expiry date on the vaccine box	Mainichi D
2005 May 31	Administration of expired polio vaccine Minoh General Health and Welfare Center	122 infants suffered no health damage	The expiry date had passed on 6 lots of vaccine, but the doctor and nurse did not check and gave oral administration with a dropper to 122 infants	Mainichi D
2005 Jun. 27	Death of female patient from major bleeding associated with catheter insertion Osaka International Cancer Center	Death of female in 50s	The catheter was inserted through a vein on the left side of the patient's neck toward the vena cava. Checking of the position showed that the tip was protruding into the left side of the thoracic cavity. When the catheter was withdrawn, major bleeding occurred and the patient fell unconscious and died shortly after	Mainichi A
2005 Jun. 28	Patient in serious condition after trachea tube misinserted into esophagus Tokyo Medical and Dental University Medical Hospital	Female in 80s fell into serious unconscious state	As a result of a trachea tube mistakenly inserted into the esophagus, the patient fell into a state of serious cerebral hypoxia	Mainichi A
2005 Jul. 7	Death of patient in 70s after vomiting blood Odate Municipal General Hospital	Death of female in 70s	When an intercostal incision was made to insert a catheter, the tip of the metal instrument caused damage to a lung blood vessel	Mainichi A
2005 Jul. 19	Patient became unconscious Tochigi Cancer Center	73-year-old male fell into serious unconscious condition	Patient from Utsunomiya awaiting cancer surgery had a catheter inserted into the right side of the chest by a male intern doctor from the surgery department, which mistakenly caused injury to the artery. The patient fell unconscious	Mainichi A
2005 Jul. 25	Patient death after bleeding overlooked following intubation of artery Sapporo City General Hospital	Patient death from multi-organ failure	Succession of mistakes in catheter insertion and subsequent treatment led to the death of a hospital patient	Mainichi A

(continued)

Table 4.1 (continued)

Date	Accident or error Name of medical institution	Injury or harm	Content of newspaper article (extract)	Source Classification
2005 Jul. 29	Patient death due to mistake during examination Sunagawa City Medical Center	Death of 79-year-old female	During examination, it was forgotten to activate an instrument to extract oxygen, leading to patient death. As it was forgotten to turn on the machine for simultaneous air supply and extraction, the patient was unable to breathe and asphyxiated	Mainichi E
2005 Jul.	Surgery went ahead with empty drip infusion and air entered vein Tohoku University Hospital	Death of female in 50s from multi-organ failure	During drip infusion of plasma with high-speed transfusion pump, the liquid inlet port became empty but surgery went ahead and air entered the vein. The patient died 6 weeks later of multi-organ failure	Mainichi E
2005 Aug.	Patient suffered consciousness disturbance after delayed discovery of kidney bleeding immediately after surgery. Kobe University Hospital	Female in 70s left with severe consciousness disturbance	In surgery for angioplasty to a renal artery, etc., the wire of a catheter inserted into the kidney blood vessel caused injury to the kidney and the patient fell into cardiopulmonary arrest. The patient was left with severe consciousness disturbance	Mainichi A
2005 Sept. 8	Patient death from major bleeding after surgical suture came loose JA Niigata Kouseiren Uonuma Hospital	Death of 44-year-old female from heavy bleeding	After surgery to remove ovarian tumor, the patient's suture became loose and the patient died of heavy bleeding. Autopsy showed that the suture thread came loose and the cause of death was heavy bleeding from the surgical wound and the abdominal cavity	Mainichi A
2005 Sept. 22	Same syringe possibly used on two individuals in preventive inoculation at elementary school in Tokamachi City Niigata Prefecture Tokamachi City Health Support Department	Low risk of infection to elementary school pupils	Suspected use of one syringe for 2 children in a combined preventive inoculation against tetanus and diphtheria	Mainichi D
2005 Sept. 22	Misprescription of labor-inducing agent, infant death in premature birth Nerima Hikarigaoka Hospital	Infant death	Female facing premature birth was mistakenly prescribed labor-inducing drug leading to the birth of a premature baby. Intern doctor apparently made a mistake in computer entry	Mainichi F
2005 Sept.	Damage to bones around eyes in surgery Nagahama City Hospital	64-year-old female left with visual impairment	After surgery for empyema, the patient complained of visual impairment. Apparently damage had occurred to the walls of the bones around the eyes, causing double vision after surgery	Mainichi A
2005 Sept.	Patient from Aichi Prefecture underwent mastectomy after breast cancer diagnosis Aichi Cancer Center Aichi Hospital	Female in 40s was mistakenly subjected to mastectomy	Mastectomy was performed after a benign tumor misdiagnosed as breast cancer. In the original diagnosis, the possibility of a benign tumor was high. Later diagnosis gave a contradictory malignant result, but no detailed examination was performed	Mainichi G

(continued)

Table 4.1 (continued)

Date	Accident or error Name of medical institution	Injury or harm	Content of newspaper article (extract)	Source Classification
2005 Oct. 3	Breathing difficulties due to tube being wrongly connected Nihon University Hospital	Death of 58-year-old male	A nurse connected the tube of an oxygen cylinder directly to a tube inserted into the patient's trachea, leading to a sudden change in condition. The patient died on the 4th due to breathing difficulties	Mainichi B
2005 Oct. 3	Death of infant after staff failed to notice alarm indicating abnormality. Kawaguchi Municipal Medical Center	Death of 5-month-old female infant from multi-organ failure	On a pediatric ward, the nurse failed to notice an alarm indicating abnormality in patient condition and a hospitalized infant fell into cardiopulmonary arrest. The alarm could only be heard as far as the corridor	Mainichi G
2005 Oct. 12	Patient death in heart surgery after mistaken administration of 10-fold dose of anesthetic Matsudo City General Hospital	Death of 1-year-old male infant from cerebral edema	Local male child receiving heart surgery was given ten times the intended dose of anesthetic and died of cerebral edema. When operating the machine that administered the drug automatically, the anesthesiologist entered the wrong numbers	Mainichi F
2005 Oct. 13	Patient death due to insufficient oxygen via artificial respirator Nagano Red Cross Kamiyamada Hospital (Currently Kamiyamada Hospital)	Patient death from acute respiratory failure	A patient using an artificial respirator died due to insufficient supply from a liquid oxygen tank. An alarm to indicate the remaining level in the tank sounded, but the response was not appropriate	Mainichi G
2005 Oct. 13	Patient in serious condition after artificial respirator became detached during nurse absence Tohoku University Hospital	Male in 80s fell into state of temporary cardiopulmonary arrest	The artificial respirator of a patient from Miyagi Prefecture became detached. Normally a nurse is in constant attendance in the room, but was temporarily absent on the day due to a series of emergency patients	Mainichi G
2005 Oct.	Misinsertion of tube, 'hospital responsible' Kurihara Central Hospital	Male in 30s fell into state of serious unconsciousness	Strong possibility that surgeon in charge of anesthesia made a mistake in insertion into trachea of polyvinyl chloride oxygen supply tube. There was also very little communication of information between the doctor and other medical staff at times of emergency	Mainichi A
2005 Nov.	Patient death from endoscopy mistake, duodenal damage overlooked Akita University Hospital	Death of male in 70s from multi-organ failure	During ERCP examination, the duodenum connecting to the bile duct was damaged by the endoscope and contrast agent leaked through the resulting hole. However the hole was mistakenly thought to be congenital, and appropriate measures were not taken	Mainichi A
2005 Dec. 21	Patient bled to death after surgery Tottori University Hospital	Death of male in 70s	Ahead of craniotomy surgery, the doctor spent approx. 15 min on the 21st securing breathing by performing a tracheotomy, but bleeding was noted and the blood collected in the trachea and caused death by asphyxiation	Mainichi A

(continued)

Table 4.1 (continued)

Date	Accident or error / Name of medical institution	Injury or harm	Content of newspaper article (extract)	Source / Classification
2005 Dec.	Gauze left in body discovered and removed 2 days after surgery / Niigata University Medical & Dental Hospital	Male in 70s. No sequelae	The patient underwent surgery around the aorta from the heart toward the lung. However, it was found that gauze had been left behind the heart. Surgery to remove it was immediately performed with the agreement of the family	Mainichi / E
2006 Feb.	Surgical tweezers left in abdomen / Mie Prefectural General Medical Center	No health damage occurred	Tweezers (7 cm long) were left in the patient abdomen after surgery. The patient had surgery to remove them 2 days later and was discharged as scheduled	Mainichi / E
2006 Mar. 11	Death from multi-organ failure after colon mistakenly injured during surgery / Miyazaki Prefectural Nobeoka Hospital	Death of 64-year-old female	The patient was hospitalized for neurological disease. For nutritional supplementation, surgery was performed to insert a tube from the abdomen to the stomach, during which the doctor mistakenly injured the colon, causing death from multi-organ failure	Mainichi / A
2006 Mar.	Patient left unconscious after brain damage in thyroid surgery / Nagoya University Hospital	Teenage female left with brain damage	The patient had surgery to remove a thyroid tumor and afterward suffered bleeding in the throat, leading to compression of the trachea and brain damage	Mainichi / A
2006 Mar.	Death from cardiac arrest after being left unattended for 28 min / Gunma Cardiovascular Center	Death of male in 70s	The patient suffered cardiac arrest and died after receiving no attention for 28 min. The cause of death was said to be acute airway blockage due to collection of phlegm in artificial nose. The hospital had at the time set the alarm to silent	Mainichi / G
2006 Apr. 20	Death of 78-year-old patient after tube misinsertion / Fukuoka Hospital	Death of 78-year-old male	The patient died after an oxygen supply tube was mistakenly inserted into the esophagus. It was noticed that a respirator supplying oxygen to the trachea via a tube had slipped and its position was adjusted. Subsequently, patient condition worsened	Mainichi / A
2006 Apr. 24	Patient death from major bleeding during surgery / Aomori Prefectural Central Hospital	Death of male patient from hemorrhagic shock	The patient died during surgery from major bleeding. After endoscopic surgery to partially resect stomach cancer, the patient had surgery to remove stomach cancer and esophageal cancer, during which the amount of bleeding gradually increased, but the site of the bleeding could not be identified	Mainichi / A
2006 May	Patient death nine days after mistake in heart surgery due to major bleeding / Gunma University Hospital	Death of male in 70s	The heart was injured during removal of catheter after surgery, causing bleeding and subsequent death. When suturing heart, the doctor had mistakenly sewn the catheter in too	Mainichi / A

(continued)

Table 4.1 (continued)

Date	Accident or error / Name of medical institution	Injury or harm	Content of newspaper article (extract)	Source / Classification
2006 Jun. 23	Drug administration mistake due to wrong drug name being entered / Kochi Prefectural Aki Hospital	Patient death	In instructions for drug administration, the treating doctor misentered the drug name in the computer. The nurse failed to notice the mistake and went ahead with the administration. The patient later suffered a sudden charge of condition and died	Mainichi / F
2006 Jun.	Misadministration of potassium chloride / Yawatahama City General Hospital	Death of 63-year-old male	The patient died after the hospital misadministered potassium chloride. The patient suffered cardiac arrest immediately after and, despite heart massage and other emergency measures, died approx. 4.5 h later	Mainichi / D
2006 Jul. 3	Patient death following administration of anticancer agent / Tokushima Prefectural Central Hospital	Death of 71-year-old male	The patient fell into cardiopulmonary arrest and died. The hospital explained that it was very possibly an allergic reaction to anticancer agents which could not have been foreseen	Mainichi / F
2006 Jul. 12	Sudden change in condition after second anesthetic injection / Shimada Municipal Hospital	Death of 46-year-old female	Death under local anesthesia for collection of bone marrow fluid from breastbone. On the first attempt, the needle did not reach the breastbone and after a second attempt, the patient underwent a sudden change of condition and died	Mainichi / A
2006 Aug. 9	Neonate death from skull fracture / Aiiku Hospital	Death of female infant immediately after birth	An infant died immediately after birth and was found to have a skull fracture. The birth was protracted and the treating doctor had employed a forceps birth, using an instrument to grip and pull the head of the fetus	Mainichi / A
2006 Aug. 22	Breathing difficulties due to expanding subcutaneous emphysema following insufficient post-surgical examination / Toyonaka Municipal Hospital	Death of 69-year-old male	Examination and other post-surgical measures were insufficient. The patient was hospitalized for esophageal cancer treatment. After surgery, a subcutaneous emphysema grew and the patient experienced breathing difficulties and cardiopulmonary arrest. He became bedridden and died of pneumonia	Mainichi / E
2006 Aug. 24	Necrosis of esophagus after nutrient leak due to damaged tube / Kagoshima University Hospital	Patient death from multi-organ failure	After surgery to partially resect the right lung, the doctor damaged a tube when trying to remove a blockage. The administered nutrient leaked and hardened and caused necrosis of the esophagus. The resulting hole opened between the esophagus and trachea led to multi-organ failure and death	Mainichi / A
2006 Sept. 1	Severe damage to infant due to diagnostic mistake / Suita Municipal Hospital	Female child left with severe damage	As mother was close to due date, the doctor diagnosed labor pains, but an examination the next morning found the heart sound of the fetus weakened. A Cesarean section was immediately performed and the cause of the abdominal pain was found to be intestinal blockage	Mainichi / E

(continued)

Table 4.1 (continued)

Date	Accident or error / Name of medical institution	Injury or harm	Content of newspaper article (extract)	Source / Classification
2006 Sept. 26	Death due to injury to artery during examination / Toyama Red Cross Hospital	Death of male in 70s from multi-organ failure	In examination of the patient thoracic artery, the doctor mistakenly caused injury and patient death. The patient complained of chest pain and was hospitalized with suspected left-side pleurisy. When syringe was used to draw off fluid, injury to the left thoracic artery led to cardiac arrest and death from multi-organ failure	Mainichi / A
2006 Oct. 4	Death of hospital patient after neglected monitoring of blood sugar levels / Toyama Red Cross Hospital	Death of 59-year-old male	The patient had abnormally elevated blood sugar levels and died. After esophageal cancer surgery, he was given a high-calorie transfusion. He had mild diabetes but developed high blood sugar, became comatose, and died	Mainichi / D
2006 Oct. 7	Patient fell unconscious during surgery / Kochi Health Sciences Center	4-year-old male infant fell into an unconscious state	An accident during surgery caused an infant from Kochi Prefecture to suffer stroke and fall into a serious unconscious condition The cause is thought to have been that a tube from the artificial heart-lung machine entered the carotid artery	Mainichi / A
2006 Oct. 13	Systemic metastasis after lung cancer overlooked during examination / Niigata Prefectural Shibata Hospital	Patient's cancer progressed to systemic metastasis	A lung cancer shadow appearing in a chest X-ray examination was overlooked for 7 months, and symptoms worsened as it progressed to systemic metastasis	Mainichi / F
2006 Nov.	Artificial respirator became detached during examination / Kobe University Hospital	Male in 80s was left with severe brain damage	As surgery following a burst aneurysm in the right leg failed to improve the symptoms, imaging examination of the blood vessel was performed, during which the supporting trolley moved and the artificial respirator became detached for approx. 10 min	Mainichi / E
2006 Dec.	Gauze left in nose for 18 years after surgery / Niigata City General Hospital	Male in 60s. No sequelae	Hemostatic gauze used in surgery 18 years earlier was discovered. The patient had a persistent blocked nose and impaired smell. On clearing his nose, two sheets of solidified gauze appeared from the left nostril	Asahi / E
2007 Jan. 14	Patient death due to liquid food entering thoracic cavity following misinsertion of tube / Higashitokushima Hospital (Currently Higashitokushima Medical Center)	Death of female in 80s	A nurse inserted a nutrition tube through the patient's nose and fed in liquid food, but there was a sudden change in condition including a fall in blood pressure. Examination showed that the tube was inserted into the bronchial tube	Mainichi / B
2007 Feb. 20	Patient with severe heart disease suffered double accident / University of Tokyo Hospital	Teenage male fell into serious unconscious condition	A patient with severe heart disease fell out of bed, causing a tube supplying blood to the ventricular assist device to become detached. After reimplant surgery the next day, the operation of the artificial respirator was again delayed, constituting a double medical accident	Asahi / C

(continued)

Table 4.1 (continued)

Date	Accident or error / Name of medical institution	Injury or harm	Content of newspaper article (extract)	Source / Classification
2007 Feb.	Mistaken administration of hypoglycemic drug led to comatose state Gastrointestinal surgery clinic in Okayama Prefecture	84-year-old female fell into vegetative state	The patient complained of poor appetite and insomnia and was examined and admitted to hospital. The patient had hypertension but was mistakenly given a hypoglycemic drug, fell into a comatose-state, and is currently resident in a care home	Asahi D
2007 Mar. 1	Patient fell into comatose state after alarm failed to sound Nagoya University Hospital	Patient in 70s fell into comatose state	During monitoring after heart disease surgery, the patient experienced ventricular fibrillation, but the alarm of the monitor failed to sound, detection was delayed, and the patient fell into a comatose state	Asahi G
2007 Mar. 28	Infant fell out of bed Yokohama Municipal Citizens' Hospital	1-year-old male infant suffered injury requiring two stitches to the nose	The patient climbed over an 82 cm high railing, tried to climb onto a shelf adjacent to the bed, but fell, striking his nose against a surface and requiring two stitches	Asahi C
2007 Apr. 17	Patient death following detachment of respirator Gokeikai Osaka Kaisei Hospital	Death of 82-year-old male	A nurse heard the alarm of the electrocardiogram monitor and hurried to the ward to find the connection of the artificial respirator detached. When the nurse adjusted the patient's position, the connection had become detached, but she explained that she had reconnected it	Mainichi B
2007 Apr.	Sequelae from arthroplasty surgery Hakodate Municipal Hospital	Male in 30s left with sequelae of right arm paralysis	In arthroplasty on dislocated right shoulder, general anesthesia and local anesthesia above the collarbone were given, but paralysis persisted after surgery. The cause was hypothesized to be that the anesthetic had for some reason entered the subarachnoid space	Asahi A
2007 May 1	Misinsertion of trachea tube into esophagus Nagoya City Emergency Medical Service	Death of 68-year-old female from myocardial infarction. Relationship with mistake unclear	During transport of cardiopulmonary arrest patient with history of myocardial infarction, a male paramedic mistakenly inserted into the esophagus a tube normally placed into the trachea to restart breathing artificially	Asahi H
2007 May 9	Patient death after tube feeding of nutrient into trachea. Iwate Medical University Circulatory Organ Medical Care Center	Death of male in 70s	A doctor mistakenly inserted a nutrition tube into the trachea and administered nutrient, causing deterioration in breathing and death from multi-organ failure	Asahi A
2007 May	Impairment due to mistake during birth Nakatsugawa Municipal General Hospital	Female child suffered severe impairment	Despite reduced heart rate in the fetus, the midwife disconnected the heart rate measuring device and neglected to inform the doctor. The condition worsened rapidly and a Cesarean delivery was performed, but the child was left with severe impairment	Asahi E

Table 4.1 (continued)

Date	Accident or error Name of medical institution	Injury or harm	Content of newspaper article (extract)	Source Classification
2007 May	Patient death due to mistake in exchange of respirator fitting Toyama City Hospital	Death of 85-year-old female	Patient failed to regain consciousness after surgery, and a cannula was inserted into the trachea through a throat incision to secure breathing. However, when exchanging the fitting, the treating doctor mistakenly tore the trachea	Mainichi A
2007 Jun. 8	Death of 83-year-old from perforation of bowel due to mistake in endoscopic examination Seki Chuo Hospital	Death of 83-year-old male	In colonic examination in which an endoscope is inserted via the anus, the doctor tore a hole of approx. 1 cm in the wall of the sigmoid colon. The patient developed peritonitis. Surgery to repair the hole was performed, but the strain of the surgery caused hospitalization. The patient died some days later	Mainichi A
2007 Jun. 10	Patient death following detachment of artificial respirator Japanese Red Cross Society Azumino Hospital	Death of female in 60s	The patient died after the tube of the artificial respirator became detached	Asahi C
2007 Jun.	During surgery, failure to notice empty drip infusion allowed air to enter cerebral artery Osaki Citizen Hospital	Death of 40-year-old female from cerebral circulatory failure	During cerebrovascular surgery, it was not noticed that the physiological saline pack of the drip infusion had become empty, and air entered the cerebral artery. The patient died of air embolism leading to cerebral circulatory failure	Asahi E
2007 Jun.	Laparoscopic surgery mistake Yamaguchi Prefecture Grand Medical Center	Female in 50s. No danger to life	Laparoscopy was performed for prolapsed womb and cystic ovarian tumor, during which the blood vessels to the ovaries were tied and cut, but a different blood vessel was accidentally damaged. The procedure was immediately switched to laparotomy and the blood vessel reconnected	Asahi A
2007 Jun.	Home visit nurse damaged urinary tract during catheter insertion Kasugai City, Aichi Prefecture	73-year-old male hospitalized for 10 days. No danger to life	When exchanging a tube into the urinary tract, the nurse damaged the urinary tract by expanding within the narrow urinary tract a balloon catheter designed to be expanded within the bladder. The patient was hospitalized and surgery given to repair the bladder fistula	Asahi B
2007 Jul. 4	Failure to notice alarm, temporary cardiopulmonary arrest Yokohama Cerebrovascular Medicine Center	Male patient suffered temporary cardiopulmonary arrest	A nurse failed to notice the alarm indicating abnormality in the patient condition and the patient suffered temporary cardiopulmonary arrest	Asahi G

(continued)

Table 4.1 (continued)

Date	Accident or error / Name of medical institution	Injury or harm	Content of newspaper article (extract)	Source / Classification
2007 Jul. 4	Death of unconscious patient from heart failure / Hikone Municipal Hospital	Death of female in 70s from heart failure	The doctor had trouble inserting an artificial respiration tube, causing sustained hypoxia in the unconscious patient and death from heart failure. The hospital claimed the cerebral hypoxia was not directly connected to the cause of death	Asahi / A
2007 Jul. 5	During dental treatment, cardiac arrest occurred under general anesthesia / Akebono Medical Welfare Center	Death of 9-year-old girl	As a child with a disability certificate was disruptive, general anesthesia was given for tooth decay treatment, but she suffered a sudden cardiac arrest. Resuscitation restored the heartbeat, but another cardiac arrest occurred at the hospital the patient was transferred to and she died	Mainichi / E
2007 Aug. 27	Patient death in special nursing home possibly due to misinsertion of nutrition tube / Elderly care home in Okayama	Death of 72-year-old male	After having a nutrition tube inserted, the patient experienced breathing difficulties and died approx. 2 h later. The tube, which should normally lead into the stomach, had entered the lung at the time of death	Mainichi / A
2007 Aug. 30	Confusion between disinfectant solutions / Hino Municipal Hospital	Three patients suffered second-degree burns to the face and mouth	When separating the surgical disinfectant Diamitol 0.025% solution into single-use portions, it was confused with a bottle containing 10% solution used for instrument disinfection. The pharmacist neglected to check the concentration	Asahi / D
2007 Aug.	Patient death following injury to blood vessel during catheter insertion / Muroran City General Hospital	Death of 70-year-old male	A blood vessel was injured when a catheter was inserted into the thigh artery and a tube to widen the blood vessel was passed through the left iliac artery. The patient died of bleeding-induced shock	Asahi / A
2007 Aug.	Benign tissue misinterpreted as malignant / Niigata Cancer Center Hospital	Female left with sequelae of numbness at surgical site	In histopathological examination of patient with suspected breast cancer, the result was misinterpreted as malignant. Part of the left breast was removed, but no malignant tumor found. Examination showed strong possibility of mistaken patient identity	Asahi / F
2007 Aug.	Tube left in abdomen / Tottori Prefectural Central Hospital	Female in 60s. No health damage	Patient in 60s who underwent surgery was discharged with 7 mm diameter medical tube still in abdomen	Asahi / E
2007 Aug.	Patient death due to insufficient transfusion during surgery / Wakkanai City Hospital	Death of female in 70s	Bleeding from the hepatic vein occurred during surgery to partially resect the liver. Transfusion was carried out using blood prepared for the purpose, but as the bleeding was heavy, damage occurred to the brain, which did not receive enough blood, and death ensued	Asahi / A

(continued)

Table 4.1 (continued)

Date	Accident or error Name of medical institution	Injury or harm	Content of newspaper article (extract)	Source Classification
2007 Aug.	Patient suffered visual impairment in empyema surgery Yokosuka City Hospital	Male in 60s left with visual impairment	In empyema surgery, a device to extract pus from the nasal recess accidentally caused injury to the muscle controlling inward movement of the left eyeball. The patient suffered visual impairment in the form of squint and double vision	Mainichi A
2007 Aug.	Part of tube left in abdomen, apology to patient Gunma Prefectural Cancer Center	No danger to patient life	The tip cover of a tube inserted during surgery to remove ascites, etc., became detached and was left behind in the abdomen. The patient complained of pain after surgery and an examination revealed the foreign object	Asahi A
2007 Sept. 18	Hospital patient had a fall and was left with paralysis Tokushima Prefectural Central Hospital	81-year-old male left with paralysis	Intestinal blockage was diagnosed and drip infusion treatment given. The nurse heard a noise from the toilet and found the patient collapsed together with the mobile drip infusion stand. He was diagnosed with external trauma-induced subarachnoid bleeding	Mainichi G
2007 Sept.	Unnecessary breast cancer surgery Niigata Cancer Center Hospital	Female in 40s had right breast removed	Benign breast cancer was misinterpreted as malignant, and the patient had part of the right breast removed	Asahi A
2007 Oct. 5	Patient died 2 h after examination Iwate Prefectural Kuji Hospital	Death of male in 70s	Approx. 2 h after undergoing an examination known as sternal aspiration to sample bone marrow fluid from the breastbone with a needle, the patient fell into hemorrhagic shock and died	Asahi A
2007 Oct. 29	Patient death due to misattachment of tube Minato Medical Coop-Kyoritsu General Hospital	Death of 89-year-old female	A tube inserted into the throat of a patient with a tracheotomy was used to extract phlegm, but a mistake was later made with the attachment fitting of the tube. As a result the patient was able to breathe in but not out, but the staff left the ward without checking	Asahi A
2007 Nov. 16	Gauze left in patient's body Yokohama Municipal Citizens' Hospital	Female was hospitalized for 6 weeks longer than scheduled	Surgery was given to transplant bone from the right ilium to the right forearm. After surgery, an X-ray carried out due to poor healing of the surgical site showed a 30 cm^2 sheet of gauze left behind	Asahi E
2007 Nov. 29	Air entered blood vessel due to misoperation of instrument Nara Prefectural Mimuro Hospital	64-year-old male left with damage and classified as having a Class 1 disability	During imaging examination of an artery in the patient's left leg, misoperation of the instrument allowed air to enter the blood vessel. The patient immediately fell unconscious and suffered a stroke. He later regained consciousness, but was left with impairment	Asahi A

(continued)

Table 4.1 (continued)

Date	Accident or error Name of medical institution	Injury or harm	Content of newspaper article (extract)	Source Classification
2007 Nov.	Inappropriate measures taken with no advance explanation Nemuro City Hospital	Death of 54-year-old male	The patient was hospitalized with a hemorrhagic gastric ulcer. Following catheter examination of the heart, the doctor performed PCI during which he took inappropriate measures without previous explanation, leading to cardiac tamponade and death	Asahi A
2007 Nov.	Walking difficulties due to drip infusion mistake Ehime Prefectural Niihama Hospital	Male in 70s infected with hepatitis B virus	During surgery to replace an abdominal blood vessel with an artificial one, the doctor failed to notice that the test result for the transfusion blood was 'pending' and proceeded with the transfusion, resulting in infection with the hepatitis B virus	Asahi F
2007 Dec. 17	Patient death after respirator left unattached Tokushukai General Hospital	Death of 87-year-old female	The artificial respirator was detached while a nurse wiped the patient's body and the nurse left the room without reattaching it. The nurse returned approx. 1 h later to find the patient collapsed and confirmed death	Mainichi B
2007 Dec. 17	Patient death due to excessive drug dose Gifu Prefectural Tajimi hospital	Death of 54-year-old male	The doctor instructed that a drug meant for administration once every 4 weeks was to be given for 3 weeks continuously. The pharmacist was dubious but did not check. The day after the last administration, the patient suffered a sudden change of condition and died some days later of bacterial pneumonia	Asahi D
2007 Dec.	Pain and numbness after treatment due to wrong injection site Tottori Prefectural Central Hospital	Male was left with damage in all limbs in the form of numbness and weakness	To relieve neck pain, the patient underwent treatment to inject drug into a nerve root in the neck. However, because the treating doctor mistakenly injected into the spine at the back of the nerve root, the patient was left with damage after surgery including numbness and weakness	Asahi A
2008 Feb. 8	Transfusion mistake due to inadequate night-time check and mistake in computer entry Oki Hospital	Death of male patient	A test engineer carried out a compatibility test on 4 packs of a stored blood preparation. In the computer entry, 'compatible' and 'non-compatible' were confused in the case of 2 of the packs	Asahi F
2008 Feb. 15	Patient fell into serious condition and had cardiac arrest during dialysis after tube became detached Omigawa General Hospital	Death of 66-year-old male	A tube returning blood from the patient's dialysis device became detached, leading to temporary cardiac arrest. The patient remained unconscious and died while still attached to the artificial respirator	Asahi G

(continued)

Table 4.1 (continued)

Date	Accident or error / Name of medical institution	Injury or harm	Content of newspaper article (extract)	Source / Classification
2008 Feb. 20	Drug administration to wrong patient / Hyogo Prefectural Kofu Hospital (Currently Hyogo Prefecture Hyogo Mental Health Center)	No change in physical condition of 65-year-old male	Nurse mistakenly gave the patient a psychotropic drug intended for another patient. Afterwards, the patient fell asleep due to the effect of the drug, but recovered with drip infusion	Mainichi B
2008 Feb.	Lung cancer overlooked in examination / Kagawa Prefectural Central Hospital	Death of female in 50s	Despite two examinations, lung cancer was overlooked. The lung cancer was later detected at another hospital. At that point, the hospital acknowledged that the result had been left unacted upon, but this was not communicated to the patient, who continued treatment	Asahi F
2008 Mar. 14	Patient death after surgery / Aomori Prefectural Asunaro Rehabilitation and Welfare Center	Death of 11-year-old girl	The patient underwent functional restoration surgery to stretch the muscles and tendons. Four doctors took part in the surgery, during which a state of cardiopulmonary arrest occurred. After treatment, the patient stabilized temporarily, but again suffered arrhythmia and died	Asahi E
2008 Apr. 1	Corneal damage due to surgical mistake resulted in reduced visual strength / Hyogo Prefectural Tsukaguchi Hospital (Now closed)	Patient suffered marked reduction in visual strength	During surgery to cauterize and block a tube connecting the right eye and nose using a high-frequency electric current, a heat-insulating seal attached to all but the tip of the needle came loose, but the doctor failed to notice and proceeded to use it. The patient suffered reduced visual strength	Mainichi A
2008 Apr. 22	Stomach tube mistakenly inserted into patient trachea / Nagasaki University Hospital	No sequelae	A treating doctor in his 20s mistakenly inserted a gastric tube for nutrient administration into the trachea. On two occasions, a total of approx. 300 cc of nutrient apparently entered the patient's lung	Asahi A
2008 Apr. 27	Death of patient and fetus reported as irregular deaths / Shizuoka Welfare Hospital	Death of mother and fetus	Ultrasound examination showed fetal heartbeat arrest and symptoms of premature separation of the placenta. The fetus was delivered by Cesarean section but died. The mother also suffered major bleeding during surgery, blood pressure fall, and death	Asahi A
2008 May 23	Drip infusion resulted in one death and abnormalities in 13 patients in the form of abdominal pain and fever / Hospital in Mie Prefecture	Of 14 patients receiving drip infusion, one 73-year-old female died	The total number of patients was 14. Identical symptoms were noted including abdominal pain, fever, vomiting, and trembling, and some patients showed severe symptoms including white blood cell count of less than one-sixth of normal	Asahi G
2008 May 27	Injection needle accidentally caused damage to aorta / Osaki Citizen Hospital	Death of 79-year-old male from blood loss	During treatment to remove pleural effusion from the chest with an injection needle, the doctor took insufficient care and misjudged the depth of the injection, causing injury to the descending aorta. The patient died the next day of hemorrhagic shock	Asahi A

(continued)

Table 4.1 (continued)

Date	Accident or error Name of medical institution	Injury or harm	Content of newspaper article (extract)	Source Classification
2008 May	Death following tube replacement Hirosaki Municipal Hospital	Death of female in 80s from peritonitis	The patient suffered a sudden change of condition after replacement of a gastric fistula tube, immediately after which the tube, which had been in the stomach, pierced the stomach, causing nutritional fluid to collect in the abdominal cavity, leading to peritonitis and death	Asahi A
2008 Jun. 15	Patient death due to food blockage caused by hospital meal Chigasaki Municipal Hospital	Death of 81-year-old male from respiratory failure	The patient ate with the assistance of a nurse. 15 min later, when another nurse came into the ward, the patient was in a state of respiratory arrest. When the trachea was pumped, the hospital meal was found to be causing a blockage. Intensive treatment was continued but the patient died	Asahi E
2008 Jun.	Gauze was left in patient's nose Toyama University Hospital	No sequelae	In surgery to remove a pituitary gland tumor via the nose, a sheet of gauze placed at the back of the patient's nose was left for approx. 4 months. The gauze was removed and there was no health damage	Asahi E
2008 Jun.	Patient death following mistaken administration of tenfold dose of sleeping drug Kagoshima Prefectural Oshima Hospital	Death of female in 70s	A sleeping drug was mistakenly administered at ten times the dose instructed by the doctor and the patient died several hours later. The attending physician ordered a prescription of 0.5 mg of the sleeping drug, but 5 mg was mistakenly prescribed	Mainichi E
2008 Jul. 3	Patient death after examination Hikari Municipal Hikari General Hospital	Death of 85-year-old male	A digestive medicine specialist carried out an endoscopic examination of the colon. As the endoscope contacted the intestine it caused a hole, and the patient developed breathing difficulties. His condition stabilized temporarily, but he died	Asahi A
2008 Jul. 6	Glaucoma patient underwent surgery in which the left and right eyes were not clearly distinguished University of Tokyo Hospital	No abnormality at surgical site	So as not to choose the wrong surgical site, a round mark was made on the patient's left temple. Later, the doctor in charge of disinfection treated the left eye. However, the surgeon failed to check the round mark, and performed surgery on the undisinfected right eye	Mainichi E
2008 Jul. 10	Patient became unconscious during anesthesia with no doctor present Aomori Kyoritsu Hospital	Male fell temporarily unconscious	It was planned to give general anesthesia and perform electric shock treatment to normalize the movements of the heart. However, several hours, earlier than scheduled, twice the normal dose was administered and the patient fell unconscious	Asahi D

(continued)

Table 4.1 (continued)

Date	Accident or error / Name of medical institution	Injury or harm	Content of newspaper article (extract)	Source / Classification
2008 Jul. 25	Patient death in tracheotomy reported as 'irregular death' / Fujioka General Hospital	Death of 83-year-old female	The patient was hospitalized urgently, unconscious and with arrested breathing, and placed on an artificial respirator. To facilitate respiratory management, tracheotomy was performed, during which however cardiac arrest occurred followed by death	Asahi / E
2008 Jul.	Sudden change in patient condition due to drug misadministration following mis-entry on prescription form / Kanagi Hospital	Death of 73-year-old female	The patient was given an antihyperglycemic agent in mistake for an antihypertensive diuretic and suffered a sudden change in condition. In accordance with the doctor's instructions, a member of agency staff had filled out the prescription form to send to the pharmacy on the computer, but misentered the drug name	Asahi / F
2008 Jul.	Needle left in body / Kobe City Medical Center General Hospital	Foreign object in body of male in 60s removed. No sequelae	In surgery to completely remove the prostate, the doctor left a stainless steel surgical needle (2 cm long, diameter 1 mm) beneath the bladder. Four years later it was discovered and removed in surgery	Mainichi / A
2008 Aug. 13	Paralysis caused by impact on brain during surgery / Omuta City Hospital	34-year-old male left with mild paralysis of left arm and leg	After empyema surgery, paralysis appeared in the left arm and leg. An inquiry by the in-house medical accident countermeasures committee found the cause to have been an impact on the brain during scraping of the nasal cartilage with a medical chisel	Asahi / A
2008 Aug. 24	Mistaken inspiration of carbon dioxide / Yame General Hospital	Male in 70s died of peritonitis and male in 80s of acute subdural hematoma	While one patient with colon cancer and one ambulance case were being transferred to the operating table for urgent surgery, a nurse mistakenly gave carbon dioxide to breathe. This misadministration was not directly linked to the cause of death	Asahi / B
2008 Sept. 10	Death during endoscopic surgery / Mutsu General Hospital	Death of 90-year-old female from peritonitis	The patient underwent endoscopic stone removal, but the tip of the endoscope caused duodenal injury and bleeding. Laparotomy was immediately performed as a countermeasure but death occurred from peritonitis	Asahi / A
2008 Sept.	Death from blood loss after accidental liver puncture / Chigasaki Municipal Hospital	Death of female in 60s	A respiratory surgeon inserted a drain from the chest surface, but the needle tip of the drain injured the liver and the patient died of hemorrhagic shock	Asahi / A

(continued)

Table 4.1 (continued)

Date	Accident or error Name of medical institution	Injury or harm	Content of newspaper article (extract)	Source Classification
2008 Oct. 9	Patient fell into serious condition during surgery due to trachea tube catching fire. Possible contact with electric surgical knife Matsudo City General Hospital	Death of male patient	During a throat incision with an electric surgical knife as part of surgery to insert a trachea tube, a different tube inserted earlier caught fire, causing severe burns to airway, oral cavity, and face	Mainichi A
2008 Oct. 15	Patient had temporary cardiopulmonary arrest due to misadministration of analgesic Yamanashi Prefectural Central Hospital	Strong possibility of female in 50s being left with brain dysfunction	The doctor mistook the name of the analgesic and used a strong analgesic normally used during surgery. When asking the nurse to fetch the drug, he gave the wrong instructions	Asahi F
2008 Oct. 27	Patient bled to death after endoscopic surgery Toyama Red Cross Hospital	Death of male in 50s from multi-organ failure	After undergoing surgery using an endoscopic electric surgical knife for early-stage stomach cancer, the patient experienced bleeding from the stomach, etc. In a second laparotomy procedure, the bleeding stopped but the patient lost consciousness, the symptoms worsened and he died of multi-organ failure	Asahi A
2008 Nov. 12	Death during surgery due to arterial injury Shizuoka City Shimizu Hospital	Death of 76-year-old male	When the doctor passed a guide wire into the right coronary artery of a myocardial infarction patient, it is suspected that the artery was injured and death occurred from cardiac tamponade	Asahi A
2008 Nov. 18	Patient death due to misadministration of muscle relaxant Tokushima Prefectural Naruto Hospital	Death of 70-year-old male	The adrenal medullary hormone succison and the muscle relaxant succin were confused, and the latter mistakenly used for drip infusion, leading to male patient's death	Asahi F
2008 Dec. 2	Patient death due to tube attached back to front Kure Kyosai Hospital	Death of male patient in 60s from multiple stroke	A clinical engineer attached the tube of a small blood pump back to front so that air was sent into the heart. After approx. 30 s, the tube was properly re-attached and the air that had entered the heart was removed, but the patient died	Asahi A
2008 Dec.	Death due to bursting of earlier overlooked aneurysm Kasugai Municipal Hospital	Death of 49-year-old female	The patient complained of a heavy head and had an MRI examination, but the doctor apparently overlooked an aneurysm on the imaging result and found 'nothing abnormal.' The aneurysm burst some days later, causing death	Asahi F
2009 Feb. 14	Reduced oxygen in respirators, 'no effect on patients' Tsuyama Chuo Hospital	No effect on 16 patients attached to artificial respirators	An anesthesiologist noticed reduced oxygen concentration in the artificial respirator of a patient on an intensive care ward. A check on the artificial respirators of this and 15 other patients showed that all had reduced concentrations	Asahi G

(continued)

Table 4.1 (continued)

Date	Accident or error Name of medical institution	Injury or harm	Content of newspaper article (extract)	Source Classification
2009 Feb. 15	Death from throat blockage by hospital meal Hiratsuka City Hospital	Death of 79-year-old female when throat blocked by hospital meal	The instruction had been given for the main dish to be rice porridge and any side dishes to be chopped small, but the senior nutritionist failed to notice, and the nurse who brought the meal also served it despite having seen the instruction 'soft food	Asahi E
2009 Feb. 26	Death of male patient due to mistake in endoscopic surgery Nishio Municipal Hospital	Death of 68-year-old male from acute peritonitis	The patient's condition changed suddenly after surgery. Urgent surgery was performed and a hole of approx. 1 cm was found in the duodenum. Death ensued from acute peritonitis. Suspected damage to duodenum in first operation	Asahi A
2009 Feb. 26	State of brain death after oxygen supply tube became detached during surgery Miyazaki Prefectural Nobeoka Hospital	Death of 57-year-old female	The doctor performed tracheotomy to fit an oxygen supply tube to a patient with respiratory failure, but when the patient's position was adjusted, the tube slipped and the patient's condition worsened. A state of brain death due to hypoxia ensued and the patient died	Asahi E
2009 Mar. 12	Doctor made mistake with drug administration after overlooking medical interview sheet Hyogo Prefectural Amagasaki Hospital	62-year-old male fell into temporary state of inability to converse	When the doctor injected the drug, blood pressure fell and the patient became unable to speak. The interview sheet noted previous allergic reaction to the drug, but the doctor and the nurse had both apparently failed to notice	Asahi F
2009 Mar.	Mistake in patient identity led to misdiagnosis of cancer and lung resection Osaka City General Hospital	Mistaken removal of lung of different female patient	The patient had suspected lung cancer and had a lung tissue sample taken for histopathological test. The test engineer however confused it with a sample from another cancer patient, and the patient was misdiagnosed with lung cancer and underwent surgery	Asahi F
2009 Apr. 14	Patient death following diagnostic mistake Kitakyushu Municipal Yahata Hospital	Death of male patient in 30s	The patient complained of chest pain and breathing difficulties and was taken to hospital by ambulance. On two occasions, the doctor failed to carry out the necessary examination during consultation, and the aortic dissection which was the cause of death was not discovered	Asahi A
2009 Apr.	Plastic cover left in blood vessel Yokohama Municipal Citizens' Hospital	Male in 70s. No health damage	The patient had surgery on a blood vessel below the knee in which blood flow is secured by expanding a balloon-shaped device. The balloon was however inserted with a cover still in place that should have been removed before surgery and that was left behind in the artery. The cover was later removed	Asahi A

(continued)

Table 4.1 (continued)

Date	Accident or error / Name of medical institution	Injury or harm	Content of newspaper article (extract)	Source / Classification
2009 Jun. 29	Post-surgical bleeding caused sequelae / Ishikawa Prefectural Central Hospital	Male in 40s left with paralysis	The patient underwent surgery for a disease in which deformation of the neck bones causes pain in the hands and arms. After surgery, a blood clot caused by bleeding from a neck blood vessel compressed the trachea. Sequelae remained despite urgent surgery	Asahi / A
2009 Jun.	Gauze left in patient abdomen / Toyooka Hospital	Male in 50s. No sequelae	After the surgery, the patient consulted another medical institution due to unwellness and X-ray examination showed gauze left behind in the abdomen. The patient was admitted to the hospital on the same day and had an operation to remove the gauze	Asahi / E
2009 Jul. 29	Air mistakenly introduced into vein / Fukushima Medical University Hospital	Two-year-old male child possibly left with brain damage	The patient was operated for gastroesophageal reflux. The anesthesiologist mistakenly introduced air into the vein. When it was noticed that the wrong tube had been used, the surgery was discontinued. After a resuscitation procedure, normal electrocardiogram wave was confirmed	Asahi / A
2009 Aug. 3	Gauze left in patient's abdomen / Kanagawa Cancer Center	Male in 50s made good recovery	In surgery to remove part of the stomach, the nurse miscounted the number of gauze sheets used and left one behind. The attending physician also failed to notice on a post-surgical X-ray	Asahi / E
2009 Aug. 24	Fetus born in anemic state and died / Kobe City Nishi-Kobe Medical Center	Death of one of twin fetuses	Cesarean section was decided and while a device to measure the fetal heartrate and other pre-operative data was detached, a syndrome occurred whereby the blood of one of the fetuses flows through the placenta into the other, and one of the fetuses fell into an anemic state	Asahi / E
2009 Aug. 27	Tube meant for stomach mistakenly inserted into trachea / Nagasaki University Hospital	Male developed pneumonia but recovered	A tube meant for the stomach was mistakenly inserted into the trachea, so that nutrient entered the lung and caused pneumonia. The patient convalesced	Asahi / A
2009 Aug.	Patient death due to misinsertion of catheter / St. Marianna Medical University Hospital	Death of male in 70s	A myocardial infarction patient underwent surgery to replace the aortic valve with an artificial valve. After surgery, when another doctor inserted a catheter, the tip of the catheter contacted the artificial valve, and the valve became stuck open	Asahi / A
2009 Sept.	Treatment delayed due to diagnostic mistake / Chiba Kaihin Municipal Hospital	Death of female in 40s from subarachnoid bleeding	A patient who was rushed to hospital after complaining of nausea and headache was diagnosed with hyperventilation syndrome. The next day she was taken to a different hospital and had surgery based on a diagnosis of subarachnoid bleeding, but failed to regain consciousness and was left with very severe sequelae	Asahi / A

(continued)

Table 4.1 (continued)

Date	Accident or error Name of medical institution	Injury or harm	Content of newspaper article (extract)	Source Classification
2009 Sept.	Mistake in gastric fistula surgery Nakatsugawa Municipal General Hospital	Death of female from heart failure	During gastric fistula surgery to open the abdominal wall and pass nutrition into the stomach through a tube, and during replacement of the tube, mistakes were made on two occasions, due to which the patient suffered diarrhea until June the following year	Asahi A
2009 Oct. 11	Death of inpatient, hospital acknowledged negligence Gifu Prefectural Tajimi Hospital	Death of female in 40s	The patient was hospitalized with burns to the face and head from a gas explosion. The swollen face and head caused compression of the airway, but the airway blockage was not noticed and the patient suffered hypoxic-ischemic encephalopathy and died of pulmonary edema approx. 10 months later	Asahi E
2009 Oct. 24	Burns due to ignition of electric surgical knife Osaka City University Hospital	Death of 74-year-old male due to respiratory failure	During a tracheotomy procedure on a patient with severe pneumonia, a spark from the electric surgical knife caused the trachea tube to catch fire. The patient suffered burns to the throat and died some days later of respiratory failure. The hospital judged that the burns aggravated the condition	Asahi A
2010 Jan. 29	Patient death due to blood vessel damage during surgery Aichi Cancer Center Hospital	Death of female in 60s from hemorrhagic shock	During surgery to remove part of the lung, damage occurred for some reason to the pulmonary artery and other tissues. Major bleeding led to a state of brain death. Death was confirmed after detachment of the heart-lung machine at the family's request	Asahi I
2010 Feb. 10	Both kidneys mistakenly removed Shin-Oyama City Hospital	70-year-old male treated at different hospital	In surgery on a patient with cancer of the right kidney, it is suspected that the two doctors mistakenly removed the left kidney. When the surgeons noticed the mistake they operated to put the left kidney back in place, but it did not recover its function	Asahi E
2010 Feb.	Patient death 10 days after chest surgery, possibly due to intubation mistake Kumamoto Medical Center	Death of male in 60s from cerebral hypoxia	When the patient's mouth was washed out with the trachea tube still in place, blood oxygen concentration dropped and the patient condition became critical. It was realized that the tube was in the esophagus, and death ensued from cerebral hypoxia	Asahi A
2010 Mar. 9	Expired vaccine mistakenly given to five males and females Mihara Red Cross Hospital	No health damage	Expired Japanese encephalitis vaccine was mistakenly given to five people. No health abnormality was observed, but the hospital maintained observation by testing blood	Asahi D

(continued)

Table 4.1 (continued)

Date	Accident or error Name of medical institution	Injury or harm	Content of newspaper article (extract)	Source Classification
2010 Mar. 18	Patient death due to air entering the tube of the artificial heart and lung machine Tokai University Hachioji Hospital	Death of 64-year-old female	The surgery was managed by the cardiovascular surgery department. Immediately after the artificial heart and lung machine was started, air infiltrated the tube supplying blood into the body, and the doctor discontinued surgery. The patient died without regaining consciousness	Asahi E
2010 Mar.	Instrument left in body Kizawa Memorial Hospital	Death of 56-year-old male	In surgery to make a hole in the stomach for a tube to supply nutrition and drugs, the metal instrument used was not recovered. Some days later it contacted the heart and caused death by bleeding	Asahi E
2010 Apr. 12	Excessive dose of anticancer agents caused serious condition due to mistaken doctor instructions Kyushu University Hospital Advanced Medical Center (Currently Kyushu University Center for Advanced Medicine Innovation)	Death of male in 70s from multi-organ failure	The patient received treatment with two anticancer agents. Blood test showed abnormal white blood cell and platelet counts, and the doctor then discovered that the anticancer agents had mistakenly been given at 1.5 and 2.8 times the intended concentrations	Asahi D
2010 Apr. 14	Patient was given drip infusion for a different patient, which was discontinued when the family noticed Fukushima Prefectural Ono Hospital	No abnormality in male patient	It was found that a nurse had mistakenly given a hospital patient an antibiotic drip infusion for another patient. When around half the drug had been given, the family noticed and the nurse halted administration	Asahi F
2010 Apr.	Gauze left behind, removed in reoperation Tottori Prefectural Central Hospital	Male in 30s. No health damage occurred	In empyema surgery, an ear, nose, and throat doctor left behind a sheet of gauze beneath the facial surface. Later, when the patient went to a dentist, the gauze was found and removed	Asahi A
2010 Apr.	A broken-off drill tip was sewn into the wound during fracture surgery Saga-Ken Medical Center Koseikan	No health damage	The orthopedic surgeon made a hole to insert a bolt for a bone transplant to an area of pulverized fracture, but the tip of the drill blade broke, and the wound was sewn up without staff realizing that it was still in the bone	Asahi A
2010 Apr.	Accidental fall from bed Kanagawa Cardiovascular and Respiratory Center	Death of male patient	The patient was hospitalized with a respiratory disease. Immediately after, he got up in bed during the night but accidentally fell and died some days later. He was elderly, but no special nursing system was in place	Asahi C
2010 Jun. 12	Patient death due to misattachment of medical instrument. 'Irregularity' report not made. Osaka Gyomeikan Hospital	Death of 87-year-old male	A nurse misattached an oxygen supply device. It is suspected that a large volume of oxygen was delivered into the airway, causing cardiac dysfunction and death. Also suspected that the incident was not reported to the police within 24 h	Asahi G

(continued)

Table 4.1 (continued)

Date	Accident or error / Name of medical institution	Injury or harm	Content of newspaper article (extract)	Source / Classification
2010 Jun.	Neonate death due to accident during delivery / Nagasaki Municipal Hospital (Currently Nagasaki Harbor Medical Center)	Death of neonate	Approx. 3.5 h after administration of a labor-inducing agent, the fetal heart rate was found to be weakened. Urgent Cesarean section was performed and a male child was born in a near-death state, failed to recover, and died six months later	Asahi / E
2010 Sept. 13	Patient fell into serious condition due to detachment of tube of ventricular assist device / Kyushu University Hospital	Death of patient in 50s	The patient underwent surgery to attach a ventricular assist device. A nurse was summoned urgently and found the patient unconscious with the tube of the artificial heart-blood pump detached	Asahi / G
2010 Oct.	Plastic sheet left in body after cancer surgery / Fujisawa City Hospital	61-year-old male suffered fever and inflammatory reaction	In surgery for esophageal cancer, a bag-shaped plastic sheet was left in the abdominal cavity, causing fever and inflammatory reaction after surgery. Now removed	Asahi / E
2010 Nov.	Gauze sheet left in body during lung transplant from a brain-dead donor / Okayama University Hospital	No sequelae	A count of the gauze sheets used during surgery immediately afterwards found one missing. An abnormal value was registered in a test on the patient's chest, and a chest CT scan showed a shadow thought to be the gauze inside the pericardium	Asahi / E
2010 Nov.	Heavy bleeding during liver surgery / Hyogo Prefectural Amagasaki Hospital	Death of 57-year-old male from multi-organ failure	The patient was diagnosed with liver cancer and underwent surgery for partial resection of the liver. The surgeon failed to suture the hepatic vein and take other measures, causing heavy bleeding. Despite hemostasis measures, the patient died 1 week later	Asahi / A
2010 Unknown	Gauze left in body / Yamagata Prefectural Kahoku Hospital	Foreign object found in body of female in 50s	Gauze was left behind for 25 years and rediscovered in abdominal surgery. Apparently it was left behind in appendix surgery at Kahoku Hospital in 1985	Asahi / A
2011 Jan. 18	Patient of blood type B left in serious condition after receiving transfusion of type A blood / Osaka City University Hospital	Male in 50s fell into serious condition	To stop bleeding from a venous aneurysm, treatment was given to inject a drug to harden the blood vessel, during which heavy bleeding and a state of shock occurred requiring transfusion. A different patient's transfusion was used, resulting in hemolytic reaction	Asahi / F
2011 Feb. 7	Patient death due to intern doctor forgetting procedure / Yaizu City Hospital	Death of 88-year-old male	An incision was made in the throat for intubation, which was changed every 2 weeks. An intern doctor assisted the nurse to do this, but mistakenly left the inner cylinder of the tube in place. The patient became unable to breathe and died	Asahi / E

(continued)

Table 4.1 (continued)

Date	Accident or error Name of medical institution	Injury or harm	Content of newspaper article (extract)	Source Classification
2011 Apr. 1	Patient death after sudden change in condition following misdiagnosis and treatment delay Tottori Prefectural Kosei Hospital	Death of 72-year-old male	The patient had surgery to remove the colon, but his condition changed suddenly with diarrhea, vomiting, etc. From the symptoms, the gastroenterological surgeon diagnosed bowel inflammation due to infectious disease and the patient was given antibiotics but developed peritonitis and died	Asahi A
2011 Apr.	Patient death after cancer was left unoperated for 3 years Nagoya University Hospital	Patient in 30s suffered cancer metastasis and death	Suspected oral cancer was diagnosed and surgery planned but not carried out for approx. 3 years. When surgery was performed, the cancer had spread to the lung and the patient died of respiratory failure. The hospital had failed to give notice of the planned date of surgery	日経 F
2011 May	Death of patient who failed to recover after administration of drug to stop bleeding Tosei General Hospital	Death of male in 80s	The patient had had a stroke and been prescribed an anticoagulant, but the coagulation function was reduced and bleeding increased so the dose was halved. A drug was administered to bring about recovery, but the bleeding did not stop and the patient died	Asahi D
2011 Jun.	Nerve damage during surgery leaves sequelae Ayabe City Hospital	Female in 80s left with sequelae including numbness in the legs	Nerve damage occurred during an operation to implant artificial bone in the patient's right leg. The patient was left with walking difficulties	Asahi A
2011 Aug. 13	Patient death due to suspected failure to remove needle Japanese Red Cross Ishinomaki Hospital	Death of female in 50s	Death after male doctor forgot to remove needle from pericardium of patient. Although the female doctor who diagnosed death due to breast cancer recognized it as a case of irregular death by medical accident, it was not reported to the police	Mainichi A
2011 Aug. 18	Patient suffered general paralysis after being given sedative with no doctor present. Hospital apology Kitakyushu Municipal Medical Center	72-year-old male left with systemic paralysis and consciousness disturbance	As mild consciousness disturbance was noted after surgery, the nurse gave a sedative-hypnotic injection on doctor's instructions, which was immediately followed by cessation of spontaneous breathing. Resuscitation treatment restored breathing, but cerebral hypoxia developed	Asahi E
2011 Sept. 25	Patient death after delayed diagnosis Tsuruoka Municipal Shonai Hospital	Death of 54-year-old male from cerebral hypoxia	Patient underwent surgery for subarachnoid bleeding, but suffered cardiopulmonary arrest. Resuscitation restored heartbeat and pulmonary edema was diagnosed, but the delay in diagnosis had a large impact on the subsequent medical condition	Asahi E

(continued)

Table 4.1 (continued)

Date	Accident or error Name of medical institution	Injury or harm	Content of newspaper article (extract)	Source Classification
2011 Oct. 12	Patient suffered partial necrosis of right arm due to leak of drip infusion Kochi Health Sciences Center	Female in 40s suffered partial necrosis of right arm	After removal of gall bladder stones, the patient was given a sedative drip infusion through the right arm. When the patient complained of feeling unwell, a blister was found at the inlet of the drip infusion, and necrosis in the surrounding tissue	Asahi E
2011 Dec. 30	Drug prescribed after allergy overlooked Emergency treatment facility in Tenri City	10-year-old boy suffered no sequelae	In consultation for cold symptoms, it was noted on the interview form that the patient was allergic to a cough medication, but the doctor and the pharmacist overlooked this and prescribed the drug. Severe allergic symptoms appeared including systemic eczema	Asahi F
2011 Dec.	Gauze left in body of patient Yamagata Prefectural Shinjo Hospital	Male in 70s. No sequelae	Gauze was found to have been left in the body during surgery. It was apparently discovered in X-ray examination immediately after suture and removed in a renewed laparotomy after explaining to the family	Asahi A

4.5 Edited by Division of Medical Adverse Event Prevention, Japan Council for Quality Health Care Project to Collect Medical Near-Miss/Adverse Event Information, Annual Report 2014

Sub-contents (extract)

I Current state of report

1. Project to Collect Medical Near-miss/Adverse Event Information
2. Report on Project to Collect, Analyze and Provide Medical Adverse Event Information
   (1) Registered medical institutions
   (2) Number of reports
   (3) Details of reports made by medical institutions subject to reporting requirements (by month of report)
   (4) Details of reports made by medical institutions subject to reporting requirements (by month of occurrence)
   (5) Details of reports made by participating registered medical institutions (by month of report)
3. Report on Project to Collect, Analyze and Provide Medical Near-miss Information
   (1) Registered medical institutions
   (2) Information report on number of events at all medical institutions
   (3) Number of reports from voluntarily participating medical institutions in sample information
   (4) Details of reports from medical institutions applying to register for participation in sample information…

II Current state of analysis of adverse event information

1. Outline and activities of Expert Analysis Group
   (1) Selection of themes for information to be analyzed
   (2) Information to be analyzed
   (3) Analysis system
   (4) Meetings
   (5) Expert Analysis Group meetings
   (6) Collection of follow-up information to medical adverse event information

2. Individual theme review
   (1) Medical accidents involving nurses and assistant nurses with less than 1 year's professional experience
   (2) Incidents involving tracheotomy tubes mistakenly entering subcutaneous or mediastinal spaces 3000

    (3) Incidents involving medical safety or data management in the duties of administrative staff

    (4) Incidents involving failure of appropriate drug treatment due to misidentification of generic drugs

    (5) Incidents involving signal transmission by wireless electrocardiogram monitors

    (6) Incidents involving management of milk formula and breastfeeding

    (7) Incidents involving reagents used in allergy tests for skin reactions

    (8) Incidents involving cleaning and disinfection of endoscopes

    (9) Incidents involving rapid instillation of potassium preparations

  (10) Incidents involving radiotherapy treatment at wrong site

  (11) Incidents involving misinterpretation of verbal information

3. Occurrence of recurring or similar incidents

    (1) Outline

    (2) Extravasation during transfusion to children (Medical Safety Information no. 7)

    (3) Ignition of drug substances by electric surgical knives (Medical Safety Information no. 34)

    (4) Extravasation during use of gabexate mesilate (Medical Safety Information no. 33); Vasculitis during use of gabexate mesilate (2nd Report) (Medical Safety Information no. 77)

    (5) Medical adverse event information to be shared: incidents involving dental treatment at wrong site (15th Report)

    (6) Use of unsterilized medical materials (Medical Safety Information no. 19)

    (7) Burns caused by bedbath towels (Medical Safety Information no. 46)

    (8) Inadequate checking of imaging diagnosis data sheets (Medical Safety Information no. 63)

    (9) Medical adverse event information to be shared: incidents involving opening, closure, failed connections, etc., in use of three-way stopcocks (11th Report).

Website: Japan Council for Quality Health Care, Project to Collect Medical Near-miss/Adverse Event Information, top page: http://www.med-safe.jp/.

- Information documents/Annual Report: http://www.med-safe.jp/contents/report/index.html
- Medical Safety Information: http://www.med-safe.jp/contents/info/index.html
- Public data search: http://www.med-safe.jp/mpsearch/SearchReport.action.

Afterword
Application of Resilience Management for Geopolitic of Far-East Asis Crises

In November 2017, America's President Trump made a round of visits to East Asian countries (Japan → South Korea → China, etc.). He returned home having combined discussions on security with business in the East Asian countries in line with his 'America First' slogan. In addition to promising to provide large sums in aid and to purchase interceptor missiles and the latest fighter planes, Japan arranged for President Trump to meet with victims of abduction to North Korea and their families, proclaiming to the world its mistrust of that country, and guaranteed its basic support in the event of a war crisis. But is this strategy really to the benefit of Japan's crisis management? As video images of the abductees were presented to the world alongside the Japan-US joint declaration, it will be difficult going forward for North Korea to acknowledge the fact of the abduction, the result of which will undeniably be to set back the possibility of a return home for the victims.

Actually, North Korea has a detailed grasp of the world situation and follows closely worldwide news and expert opinion. Armed with this knowledge, it may well be that it chooses to fly in the face of the international community by deploying strategies designed to outsmart the response strategies of player nations. North Korea has already carried out successful nuclear tests, and—setting aside the debate as to whether Japan should allow itself to acquire a nuclear capability—a threat of nuclear development and long-range missiles focused on the seas around Japan has grown into an international issue. At present, in addition to the tactic of indirectly encircling North Korea through regional diplomacy, the crisis management strategy for guaranteeing the security of Japan and East Asia through the nuclear disablement of North Korea is one of nuclear deterrence against North Korea by engaging Russia—a stakeholder in the sea area around Japan, where the risk of hostilities is highest—in direct negotiations through military exercises and other contacts, backed by the American promise to station attack submarines carrying nuclear weapons in the Japan Sea.

From a resilience viewpoint, the strategy for war avoidance is direct negotiation with stakeholder nations (Russia, China) around the envisaged crisis and maintenance of diplomatic channels along the axis of conflict. In the case of a military near miss between North Korea and the US army leading to war, the only party that can intervene between them is probably Russia's President Putin. We must not forget the history of past wars, in which trivial near misses have developed into war, and as a result of diplomatic channels being abandoned, wars that were meant to end immediately have been prolonged, leading to great misery. Japan's prime minister is working to win the understanding and cooperation of neighboring countries including India, but surely he should not have an exaggerated expectation that overseas nations share the fossilized oriental values of the far-eastern country which is Japan. Looking at the group of stakeholder nations in this area, the directly involved parties Japan and South Korea are the objects of the crisis, while for Russia and China the related strength of the risk is high, and for America the military, economic, and political advantage to be gained from an intervention is not great. Applying the approach of Japan's inward-looking social organization to the wider world will not lead to problem resolution, as demonstrated by history. Looking at its domestic situation, the number of suicides is high as a proportion of the population at over 30,000, while deaths and suicides from overwork are also high, so that every year the United Nations gives the recommendation that Japan's long working hours should be curtailed. Given Japan's falling birth rate and aging society, the social practice of unpaid overtime, which has no international parallel, and the structural inertia and spiritual ethos of its organizations can be seen as dangerous phenomena posing enormous latent risk. For problem resolution in the near future, it may be necessary to explore the potential of resilience techniques and concrete prescriptions.

Casting our minds back, we see that the process by which the Imperial Headquarters in the Second World War disguised defeat as victory and thus hid the true situation of the war from the people is reflected in the repeated cases among contemporary enterprises of data falsification, secretive recalls, corporate scandals, leaking of customer names, and other such incidents of social damage through the opposition between internal reality (*honne*) and public façade (*tatemae*). These expose the strengths and failings of Japan's rigidly organized society. Expansion into overseas markets meanwhile has tended to flow all at once in the same direction, from China to southeast Asia then India and so on, leaving Japanese businesses vulnerable to insufficient production capacity at the time of the great floods in the Mekong Delta and the expulsion of Japanese-owned enterprises from China due to anti-Japanese activities. Thus, not only are natural disasters frequent, so also are human-made disasters. As seen in the Fukushima nuclear accident, which arose from an unforeseen natural disaster, natural and human-made disasters are connected, and Japan's situation therefore assigns to it a duty to lead the world in exploring crisis management and resilience aimed at disaster reduction. At the abovementioned ISSS workshop, I pointed out that the medical care, welfare, public health, long-term care, and pension systems are vulnerable to the global risk posed by falling birth rates and social aging, and made proposals on disaster reduction research to reduce the medical accidents which are a shared problem of the developed countries and guarantee sustainability. I enjoyed the support of Professors G. Chroust and S. Sankaran.

As became clear in the 2011 Great East Japan Earthquake, if rescue and first aid are not sufficient in a large-scale national disaster, the cooperative action of the local community becomes important; People: road, rail, and air transport links (airfields) were cut and emergency equipment and supplies did not reach the necessary areas; Material: donations from across the country were not delivered to the disaster zone and their distribution was held up, while government measures for the disaster zone were also delayed so that individual local authorities were left to their own devices; Money: earthquake forecast systems completely failed to function, and crisis management immediately after the disaster was also inadequate; not only with reference to the earthquake but also the public evacuation order following the Fukushima nuclear disaster, disclosure of information to the public cannot be described as sufficient; Information: from the first 36 h of first aid and life-saving and throughout the recovery and reconstruction phase of housing construction, local economic revival, and employment creation, the dispersed local community, particularly families of the rising generation, became uncertain with the passing of time about whether to return to the disaster zone; Time: as illustrated above, after people, material, money, and information, the next most important resources were the effective use of limited time plus the spirit of mutual assistance among people in the form of community ties, which were reported to have limited the spread of the disaster and thus had a disaster reduction effect. Particularly in Japan, with the importance of public facade, there is a strong tendency to report only what sounds positive, which weakened the ability to identify the true situation. To prepare for the next generation by transmitting reality as it is without distortion and learning its lessons for future benefit, we need to see not only the bright side, but also confront the dark side. That is where disaster reduction (disaster management) begins.

Regarding the situation on the Korean Peninsula, which is one of Japan's neighboring countries, China, Russia, America, and the countries of East Asia are moving from sanction measures against North Korea's nuclear and missile development to active opposition measures. Overseas countries fear that Japan may respond against North Korea by acquiring nuclear weapons. If it came to a war in the Japan Sea (East China Sea), which is now the world's most unstable area, it is estimated that a limited conflict would claim 20 million victims, and a nuclear conflict more than 200 million (author's estimate). After the war, nearly five million refugees would, as in Afghanistan, Iraq, and Syria, flow across borders, bringing the danger of frequent terrorism in Asia. In August to November 2017, following the deployment of the US aircraft carrier USS Carl Vinson, three further nuclear-powered aircraft carriers—the USS Ronald Reagan, Theodore Roosevelt, and Nimitz—were sent to the Japan Sea and the western Pacific Ocean, demonstrating military power to North Korea, China, and Russia. For countries close to the development of a hydrogen bomb and possessing ballistic missiles with nuclear capability, the deterrent effect lies, as in the US-Russian cold war, in the nuclear offensive submarines which can penetrate their inshore waters. Decisive for large nuclear submarines, which carry 24 nuclear missiles, is not only their ability to launch a preemptive strike in the event of a crisis, but also the ability to inflict retaliatory damage. To resolve the instability in the Korean Peninsula, an urgent issue for the guarantee of security in the Asian Far East is the permanent presence in the Japan Sea of US army nuclear attack submarines. The consensus in the Asian region is that war must be avoided at all costs.

The stance of each country toward the situation in East Asia is summarized below (Table A.1).

Table A.1 Resilience management 2017–18 for the crisis of East-Asian sustainability

National interests	Stage		
	Risk	Crisis	Resilience
America	Interests in Asia-Pacific sea areas Display of force to the world with military exercises using aircraft carriers System ×, leadership ×	Damage to US army bases in Japan, military bases in Guam, Hawaii Nuclear submarines able to reach Korean Peninsula	No benefit from war. Shift to trading and economic relationship and military supplies business with countries of East Asia
Russia	Interests in North Pacific sea areas including Sea of Okhotsk, Arctic Sea, and northern Japan Sea and buffer zone with western sphere of influence System ○, leadership ○	Instability in Russian Far East (Vladivostok, Nakhodka, Aleutian Islands, Kuril Islands)	Careful monitoring of American response, higher profile in international opinion (criticism over Crimea/Ukraine; Cuba policy)
China	In event of emergency, conflict at China-North Korea border and in surrounding sea areas. Possible loss of buffer zone with western and Russian spheres of influence System ○, leadership ×	Instability of China-North Korea border, tension in East China and Japan Sea areas. Reluctance to intervene of Russia and America. Damage to Pacific expansion	After Korean Peninsula crisis, North Korean refugees, as in Afghanistan, Iraq, and Syria, risk becoming incubators of Asian terrorism
North Korea	Maintain the domestic system of control through media-led focus of public attention on risk of unpredictable military provocation by America, South Korea, Japan, China	In event of fall of Kim dynasty, possibility of ensuing collapse of both country and system. Weak organizational control over armed forces, disorderly military conduct, rioting	North Korean refugees and leaders have nowhere in world to escape to. Leave communication channels open, friendly nations Russia, Iran
South Korea	38th Parallel and Seoul are close, risk increasing. Clear distancing from	Quarrels within Korean Peninsula between nations of same ethnicity risk escalating from near	Scenario for crisis avoidance unclear

(continued)

Table A.1 (continued)

National interests	Stage		
	Risk	Crisis	Resilience
	American support and Japan, but policy unclear. System ○, leadership ×	misses at front line into war	Policy inconsistent from government to government
Japan	Late response along route of North Korea missile tests. Reliance on America to guarantee security on land and in Japan Sea area, purchase of anti-missile weapons. System ×, leadership ×	Diplomatic efforts with surrounding countries may prove ineffective in a crisis. Encircling tactic to isolate North Korea under guise of pressure and dialog may induce and intensify war	Risk avoidance measures are inadequate, weak preparation for event of crisis, no vision for resilience. Essential to consider possible consequences of crisis and create international response
India	If no risk and no threat from war or other crises, may grow into world-level Asian economic power System −, leadership ×	Possibility of East Asian instability affecting not just Japan Sea area and China-North Korea border but sparking trouble on China-India border	Advent of opportunity to prosper within commercial sphere of China, which is Asian leader in global economy. May challenge China's trade interests with America and EU
EU nations	Apprehension over risk to East Asian economy, which is linked to EU economy. Concern over issues arising from refugee flows from military conflict System ×, leadership ×	Balance of nuclear deterrence expected from American and Russian nuclear submarines in Japan Sea area. Historical background of EU hostility to nondemocratic countries	EU not interested in East Asia. Preoccupied instead with EU split or sharp devaluation of euro. Damage to East Asian economic area from situation on Korean peninsula may have repercussions for EU

Note The above table is a summary created by the author following discussion of the situation in East Asia with European and American researchers workshop presentation at the 2017 ISSS conference at Vienna Technical University

Bibliography

Argyris, C. and Schön, D., *Organizational Learning: A Theory of Action Perspective*, Addison-Wesley, 1978.

Argyris, C., *Integrating the Individual and the Organization*, Transaction Publishers, 1974, 1990.

Argyris, C., *Knowledge for Action*, Jossey-Bass Publishers, 1993.

Aruga, T. (edi) *Wise regulation: medical accident system investigative system*, Herusu Shuppan, 2016.

Asai, A., et al., *Medical Ethics*. Keiso Shobo, 2002.

Association for Research into Medical Errors and Problems, *Emergency line for medical issues*, Civil Law Research Association, 1997.

Association of Japanese Healthcare Corporations (edi.), *Q&A on medical accident investigation guidebook*. Chugai-Igakusha, 2016.

Atsuji, S., *Unsafety: Disaster Management, Organizational Accidents, and Crisis Sciences for Sustainability*, Springer, 2016.

Barnard, C. I., *The Functions of the Executive*, Harvard University Press, 1938, pp. 282–283.

Brennan, T. A., Leape, L. L. and Laird, N. M., "Incidence of adverse events and negligence in hospitalized patients: Results of the Harvard Medical Practice Study I", *The New England Journal of Medicine*, 324: 370–376, 1991.

Chubu-Nippon Broadcasting News: No More Medical Accidents!, Fubaisha Ltd., 2003.

Degos, L., *How errors can reduce medical accidents*, NTT Publishing, 2015.

Donaldson, L., *An Organization with a Memory: Report of an Expert Group on Learning from Adverse Events in the NHS Chaired by the Chief Medical Officer*, National Health Service, The Stationery Office, 2000.

Eunjung, C. A., "Researchers: Medical errors now third leading cause of death in United States", *The Washington Post*, May 3, 2016.

Fukuyama, M., *Medical accident finance interpreted from a doctor's perspective,* Nanzando Co., Ltd., 2011.

Funase, S., *The great medical care collapse*. Kyoei Shobo, 2016.

Furukawa, T., *How hospitals can 'kill' you*. Daisanshokan, 2002.

Fushiki, S., Katagi, N. and Shimoda, M. (eds.), *Bioethics and medical ethics. Revised 3rd Edition*, Kinpodo, Inc. 2014.

Gregory E. Pence (transl. Miyasaka, M. and Nagaok, S.): *Medical Ethics 1*. Misuzu Shobo, 2000.

Gregory E. Pence (transl. Miyasaka, M. and Nagaoka, S.): *Medical Ethics 2*. Misuzu Shobo, 2001.

Hilfiker, D., "Making medical mistakes: How doctors harm patients-and themselves", *Harper's Magazine*, Harper's, 1984.

© The Author(s), under exclusive license to Springer Nature Singapore Pte Ltd. 2019
S. Atsuji, *Resilience Management for a Sustainable Aging Society*,
SpringerBriefs in Business, https://doi.org/10.1007/978-981-13-5805-0

Hodgetts, T. H. (transl. Hase, T., et al.): *Major incident management system: scene aide memoire for medical management and support*, Nagai Shoten Co., Ltd., 2006.

Iida, S. (edi), *Guidelines on accident investigations in hospital: appropriate response at the time of accident occurrence can be traced through the timeline*, Medicus Shuppan Publishers, 2015.

Imanishi, Y., *Why medical mistakes happen*, Kenyukan, 1996.

Inoue, K., *Medical accident investigation system, legal interpretation, and administrative operation approach; Q&A*. Mynavi Publishing, 2015.

Ishii, T. (edi), *The nursing professionals who ensure patient safety*, Ishiyaku Pub., Inc., 2015.

Ishii, T., *Medical accidents from the viewpoint of nursing law and ethics. 2nd Edition*, Igaku-Shoin Ltd., 1999.

Ishikawa, H. (edi.) *The medical accident investigation system: what should happen with it and what we should do about it*. Sairosha, 2015.

Japan Council for Quality Health Care, *Iryō jiko jōhō shūshū tō jigyō heisei 27-nendonenhō*, (Medical accident data collection and other projects), Annual Report, 2015.

Japan Medical Association (edi.), *Iryōjūjisha no tame no iryō anzen taisaku manyuaru*. (Manual of medical safety measures for medical professionals), 2007.

Japanese Association for Radiation Accident/Disaster Medicine (ed.). *Fukushima Nuclear Accident: what we were able and unable to do*. Iryo Kagaku Sya, 2012.

Kamiya, K. (edi.), *Toward a new era in which medical liability and accidents are not punished and errors are not overlooked*. Mainichi Communications, 2007.

Kato, Y. (edi), *Learning from medical accidents: significance and practice of accident investigations*, Chuohoki Publishing, 2005.

Kohn, L. T., Corrigan, J. M. and Donaldson, M. S. (eds.), *To Err is Human: Building a Safer Health System Committee on Quality of Health Care in America: Institute of Medicine*, National Academy Press, 1999.

Kono, R., *Human error in medical treatment: why mistakes happen and how to prevent them. 2nd Edition*, Igaku-Shoin Ltd., 2014.

Kyoto Comparative Law Center, Medical and Legal Network (ed.), "Emerging medical accident investigation systems", *SCICUS*, 2015.

Kyoto Comparative Law Center, Medical and Legal Network (ed.), "Legal professionals and doctors explain emerging medical accident investigation systems", *SCICUS*, 2015.

Leape, L. L., Brennan, T. A. and Laird, N. M., "The nature of adverse events and negligence in hospitalized patients: Results of the Harvard Medical Practice Study II", *The New England Journal of Medicine*, 324: 377–384, 1991.

Leape, L. L., "Errors in Medicine", *JAMA*, December 21, 1994-Vol 272, No. 23, pp. 1851–1857.

March, J. G. and Cyert, R. M., *A Behavioral Theory of the Firm*, Prentice-Hall, 1963.

March, J. G. and Olsen, J. P., *Ambiguity and Choice in Organization*, Universitetsforlaget, 1976.

March, J. G. and Simon, H. A., *Organizations*; 2nd edition, Blackwell Publishers, 1993 (1st edition, 1953).

March, J. G., *Decisions and Organizations*, Basil Blackwell, 1988.

Matsumura, Y. (edi), "Accident investigation guidelines at Kyoto University", *Medical Review*, Hospital and response practice of the Medical Safety Management Department, 2016.

Matsushita, Y. (edi), *Medical Safety, 3rd Edition: Nursing Graphic: Integration and practice of nursing*, Medica Shuppan Publishers, 2015.

Mitobe, H. et al., *Eliminating medical accidents*. KI Media, 1999.

Miura, T. (edi), *Psychology of accidents and safety: risk and human error*, University of Tokyo Press, 2007.

Munakata, Y. (edi), "Lessons in risk management from accident examples", *Nursing Mook*, Gakken Co., Ltd., 2007.

Murakami, Y., *Safety Science*. Seidosha, 1998.

Muramatsu, M. (ed.), *Social science lessons from major disasters: Vol. 3. Fukushima nuclear power accident and multiple risk governance*, Toyo Keizai Inc., 2015.

Nagai, H., *Medical error incident at Tokyo Metropolitan Hiroo Hospital where 'cover-up' of a medical accident was condemned: a book written in memory of the ordeal of my wife Etsuko*, Akebi Shobo Corporation, 2007.

Nakayama, T. (edi), "Social innovation led by medical care big data", *Nikkei Business*, Nikkei Publication, 2014.

Nichigai Associates (ed.), *Accident and disaster reference book*, Nichigai Associates Inc., 2015.

Nikkei Medical (ed.), *Medical accident investigation system manual*, Nikkei Business Publication, 2015.

Nippon Koteisho Kyokai (ed.), "Toward medical accident prevention: approach from pharmaceuticals and medical instruments", *Medical information Express*, Elsevier Science, 2002.

Nishida, S., *Medical accident: a non-fiction account of the author's own experience*, Hiroenterprise, 2014.

Nishida, S., *Online documentary on the experiences of the author, who forced a university hospital to recognize its role in the occurrence of a medical accident that caused a life-and-death situation*, Hiroenterprise, 2016.

Oe, W., *Medical accident emergency response manual: crisis communication by medical institutions*, Publication department of SANRO Research Institute, Inc., 2009.

Ombudsman (ed.), *Medical accidents, medical file disclosure, and patient rights. 2nd Edition.* Akashi Shoseki, 2006.

Oshida, S., *Medical accidents: facts and problem points*, Shodensha Publishing, 2005.

Oshida, S., *Why do medical accidents happen?*, Shinyusha, 2013.

Reason, J., *Managing the Risks of Organizational Accidents.* Ashgate Publishing, 1997. (Translated by Shiomi H., Takano K., Sasō K., *Soshiki jiko: okorubekushite okoru jiko kara no dasshutsu*, JUSE Press, 2001, p. 173).

Reason, J., *The Human Contribution: Unsafe Acts, Accidents, and Heroic Recoveries*, Ashgate Publishing, 2008.

Robert M. Wachter, "Technology to reduce medical accidents", *Nikkei Business*, Nikkei Publication, 2015.

Sasaki, T. (edi), *Gendai keieigaku no kihon mondai: Basic problems of modern business management science*, Bunshindo, 1999, p. 213.

Sexton, J. B., Thomas, E. J. and Helmreich, R. L., "Error, Stress, and Teamwork in Medicine and Aviation: Cross-sectional Surveys", *BMJ*, 320: 745–749, 2000.

Silver, L. M., *Remaking Eden: How Genetic Engineering and Cloning will Transform the American Family*, Avon Books, 1997.

Simon, R., Salisbury, M. and Wagner, G., "MedTeam: Teamwork advances emergency department effectiveness and reduces medical errors", *Ambul Outreach*, Spring, 21–4, 2000.

Simon, H. A. and Langley, P., "The Central Role of Learning in Cognition", *The Models of Thought*, Yale University, 1989, pp. 102–115.

Simon, H. A. and Newell, A., *Human Problem Solving*, Prentice-Hall, 1972.

Simon, H. A. and Prietura, M. J., "The Experts in Your Middest", *Harvard Business Review*, Jan.–Feb. 1989, pp. 120–124.

Simon, H. A., *Administrative Behavior: A Study of Decision-Making Processes in Administrative Organizations*, Macmillan Publishing, 1945 (3rd edition, The Free Press, 1976).

Simon, H. A., *Models of Thought, Vol. 3*, Yale University, 1979, pp. 30–38.

Simon, H. A., Newell, A. and Shaw, J. C., "Elements of a Theory of Human Problem Solving", *Psychological Review*, 1958, Vol. 65, pp. 151–166.

Simon, H. A., *Reason in Human Affairs*, Stanford University Press, 1983.

Simon, H. A., "Rational Choice and the Structure of the environment", *Psychological Review*, Vol. 63, 1956, pp. 129–138.

Simon, H. A., "Simulation of Cognitive Processes; A Report on the Summer Research Training Institute", *Social Science Research Council*, 1953, Vol. 12, pp. 37–40.

Simon. H. A., *The Science of the Artificial*, MIT Press, 1985.

Sims, H. P., Gioia, D. A. and associates (eds.), *The Thinking Organization; Dynamics of Organizational Social Cognition*, Jossey-Bass, 1986.

Tanigawa, K. (eds.), *Witness statements from doctors and medical response record of the Fukushima Daiichi Nuclear Power Plant accident*. Herusu Shuppan, 2013.

Watanabe, S. and Yoshikawa, A., *Japan's medical care crisis*, Gentosha, 2015.

Yamauchi, K. and Yamauchi, T., *How medical accidents happen and how to prevent them*. Asahi Shimbun Company, 2000.

Yamauchi, K. and Yamauchi, T., *Iryō jiko (Medical accidents)*, Asahi Shimbun Company, 2000, p. 102.

Yasufuku, K., *Why an innocent doctor was arrested: Ohno Hospital: the trial that changed the history of medical accident trials*. Hojosha, 2016.

Yui, Y., *Risk management for medical accident prevention*. Igaku Geijutsusha, 2001.

Index

© The Author(s), under exclusive license to Springer Nature Singapore Pte Ltd. 2019   133
S. Atsuji, *Resilience Management for a Sustainable Aging Society*,
SpringerBriefs in Business, https://doi.org/10.1007/978-981-13-5805-0